DK EYEWITNESS TRAVEL

TOP 10
SEATTLE

ERIC AMRINE

Top 10 Seattle Highlights

The Top 10 of Everything

CONTENTS

Seattle Area by Area

Streetsmart

Within each Top 10 list in this book, no hierarchy of quality or popularity is implied. All 10 are, in the editor's opinion, of roughly equal merit. Throughout this book, floors are referred to in accordance with American usage; i.e., the "first floor" is at ground level.

Front cover and spine *The Space Needle, Monorail and EMP Museum Building in Seattle*
Back cover *The dramatic cityscape of Seattle, as viewed from Kerry Park*
Title page *Native American art from Seattle*

Welcome to
Seattle

Maybe the city learned its ambition from the salmon, who migrate through the city center, battering themselves on the rocky riverbed. Maybe the trees that define the Pacific Northwest landscape taught Seattle to reach high, made it home to airplanes, computer science, and art. Whatever it was, Seattle is now one of the United States' fastest growing cities. With Eyewitness Top 10 Seattle, it's yours to explore.

Stunning scenery surrounds the city. To the west of downtown's skyscrapers are the waters of **Puget Sound** and the peaks of the **Olympic Mountains**. From the observation deck in **Columbia Center** or the **Volunteer Park Water Tower**, you can see the **Cascade Mountains** to the east. Surrounding downtown are seven different neighborhoods, each with its own district character, including **Capitol Hill**'s vibrant LGBTQ scene, **Ballard**'s celebration of its Scandinavian roots, and **West Seattle**'s beachy vibe.

The totem poles in **Pioneer Square** – and other places throughout the city – remind visitors that Native American people were here long before Western settlers claimed the land. Geography limits the city; imagination does not. The **Amazon headquarters'** glassy globes and the striking architecture of the **Central Library** show a city racing for the future, while shoppers still buy produce from the 100-year-old **Pike Place Market**.

Whether you are visiting for a weekend or a week, our Top 10 guide brings together the best of everything that Seattle has to offer. You will find everything from the city's best festivals to jazz and grunge nightlife spots. There are suggestions for local dive bars, farm-to-table dining, and exceptional places to stay, too. Useful tips feature throughout, from seeking out what's free to avoiding the crowds, plus seven easy-to-follow itineraries. Add inspiring photography and detailed maps, and you have the essential pocket-sized travel companion. **Enjoy the book, and enjoy Seattle**.

Clockwise from top: Downtown Seattle; totem pole, Pioneer Square; Pike Place Market; West Point Lighthouse; Space Needle, Seattle Center; Museum of Pop Culture; Washington Park Arboretum and Japanese Garden

Exploring Seattle

Using downtown Seattle as a base, it is easy to reach the city's top attractions on foot or via public transit. A few of them are in the outer neighborhoods, all readily accessible by bus, but the freedom of a car for the day may be enjoyable. Keeping orientated is easy – the waters of Puget Sound will always be to the west.

The instantly recognizable **Space Needle** dominates the high-rise skyline in downtown Seattle.

Key
- Two-day itinerary
- Four-day itinerary

Two Days in Seattle

Day ❶
MORNING
Visit the stalls at **Pike Place Market** *(see pp12–13)*, and watch out for the flying fish at the Pike Place Fish Company! Grab coffee at Starbucks – the original store is located here.

AFTERNOON
Ride the monorail from Westlake Plaza to **Seattle Center** *(see pp14–15)* for a trip up the iconic Space Needle. Afterwards, record a future hit single at the Museum of Pop Culture.

Day ❷
MORNING
Meet the critters that live in Puget Sound at the Seattle Aquarium then shop for souvenirs along the **Seattle Waterfront** *(see pp16–17)* before having a seafood lunch.

AFTERNOON
Go underground in **Pioneer Square** *(see pp18–19)* to learn the colorful history of Seattle's early settlers. Above ground, take time to see the totem poles in Occidental Park.

Four Days in Seattle

Day ❶
MORNING
Take a stroll in the historic grounds of the **University of Washington** (UW) *(see pp28–9)*. Visit the Henry Art Gallery on campus for contemporary art and stop at the Washington Park Arboretum *(see p47)*.

AFTERNOON
Capitol Hill *(see pp78–85)* is Seattle's hottest bar and restaurant district and the heart of Seattle's LGBTQ population. Fuel up with coffee, then catch a live show or dance at one of the neighborhood's inclusive clubs.

Day ❷
MORNING
Make the worthwhile trip to **Discovery Park** *(see pp32–3)* for a hike and the spectacular views of the Olympic Mountains. Bus 33 from downtown Seattle takes you to Fort Lawton on the bluffs above Puget Sound.

AFTERNOON
In summer and fall, stop at the Fish Ladder on **Lake Washington Ship**

Discovery Park offers stunning views over Puget Sound towards Mount Rainier, Washington State's highest peak.

Around Seattle

Lake Washington Ship Canal
Woodland Park Zoo
University of Washington
BUS 33
Discovery Park
Bainbridge Island
BUS 5
Capitol Hill
FERRY
Area of main map
Puget Sound
BUS
0 km   4
0 miles   4
Museum of Flight

for some window shopping and an ice cream, then plan the return trip to Seattle in time for sunset.

Day ❹
MORNING
Seattle was once called Jet City for its airplane industry. Visit the barn where Boeing made its first plane at the **Museum of Flight** (see p39).
AFTERNOON
Spend the last afternoon in the historic Panama Hotel Tea House in the **International District** (see pp22–3), the center of Seattle's Pacific Rim culture. Stay in the area for dinner – there are Chinese, Vietnamese, and Cambodian options, as well as pizza places and popular cafés.

Woodland Park Zoo
BUS 5
Denny Park
MONORAIL
BUS 5
❶
❷ ❸
Westlake Plaza
Starbuck's first store
Pike Place Market
FIRST HILL
❸
BUS 5
Seattle Aquarium
Seattle Waterfront
DOWNTOWN
❷
Seattle Ferry Terminal
← Bainbridge Island
Pioneer Square
PIONEER SQUARE
Panama Hotel Tea Room
Occidental Park
❹
INTERNATIONAL DISTRICT
BUS 142
from Museum of Flight ↑
0 meters   500
0 yards   500

Canal (see pp26–7) to watch the salmon fight their way upstream. Watch fishing vessels share the water with kayakers in the Ballard Locks.

Day ❸
MORNING
Laugh at the antics of Penguins or gaze into the eyes of a gorilla at **Woodland Park Zoo** (see pp30–31). Bus 5 heads here from downtown, and there is discounted entry for those who show a valid bus ticket.
AFTERNOON
Ride a ferry to Bainbridge Island (see p65). Walk into the village of Winslow

Woodland Park Zoo is home to exotic animal species, such as this orangutan.

Top 10 Seattle Highlights

The futuristic Space Needle standing tall above the Seattle skyline

Seattle Highlights

Seattle is a powerhouse of influence, steering the future of high technology as well as popular culture with a population fueled by espresso coffee, the latest developments in software, music, and visual art. Seattle has emerged as one of the most ambitious cities in the United States, with an ever-changing skyline that reflects the pioneers who settled here in the mid-19th century.

1 Pike Place Market
An integral part of the Seattle experience, this market is famous for its mix of fresh seafood, farmers' produce, and ethnic foods *(see pp12–13)*.

2 Seattle Center

This center is dedicated to the pursuit of arts and entertainment. While many original edifices remain – the Space Needle being the most recognized – the location also inspires new designs, such as Gehry's Museum of Pop Culture *(see pp14–15)*.

3 Seattle Waterfront
The city is a major port for both industrial and passenger traffic. Along with the Seattle Aquarium, sights include shops and restaurants just blocks from cranes loading containers *(see pp16–17)*.

4 Pioneer Square
A treasure trove of Victorian-era buildings and streets paved with cobblestones, Seattle's original commercial center was established in 1852 when Arthur A. Denny and David Denny arrived with fellow pioneers *(see pp18–19)*.

5 International District
The ID, as locals call it, is a mix of Asian cultures. Seattle's Pacific Rim identity makes it a destination for those from across the Pacific *(see pp22–3)*.

6 Broadway

An evening around Broadway can resemble Manhattan in terms of liveliness. Expect the unexpected, and lots of outrageous attire and flamboyant behavior *(see pp24–5)*.

Lake Washington Ship Canal 7

Officially completed in 1934, the canal bisects the city and provides access to the sea for pleasure boaters, research vessels, and commercial barges alike *(see pp26–7)*.

8 University of Washington

One of the nation's top universities, UW comprises more than 45,000 students, an attractive campus, and endowments from benefactors in the tech industry *(see pp28–9)*.

9 Woodland Park Zoo

The design of Seattle's world-class zoo affords its animals vast enclosures. Natural habitats surround the viewing areas, and pathways snake throughout the grounds *(see pp30–31)*.

10 Discovery Park

Rising above Puget Sound is a gorgeous 534-acre (216-ha) park. Densely wooded trails, beaches, historic military homes, and wildlife are just some of its attractive features *(see pp32–3)*.

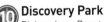

TOP 10 ⭐ Pike Place Market

The market stretches for several blocks high above the boats on Elliott Bay. This historic district includes a multilevel underground arcade, and street-level tables and stalls. First established in 1907, America's oldest farmers' market has become one of Seattle's most treasured institutions. By mid-century, most stalls were run by Japanese-Americans, and their tragic internment during World War II nearly ended the market's operation. Plans to raze the site fortunately ceased in 1971, when architect Victor Steinbrueck and his supporters saved it from the wrecking ball.

1 Hmong Flower Stalls

Seattle's small, highly entrepreneurial South East Asian Hmong community dominates the market's flower stalls **(below)**. The fresh blossoms can be smelled even before seeing them through the crowds. During the winter, residents make do with colorful dried flowers.

2 Pike Place Fish Market

Crowds and movie crews gather to witness these entertaining fishmongers **(above)**. Their skills include hurling their stock high over customers and countertops.

3 Starbucks

Steamed, frothy milk and dark roasted coffee can now be found all over the world. Howard Schultz's retail coffee empire began right here in 1971, when Starbucks opened its first store.

NEED TO KNOW

MAP J4 ■ Between Pike & Virginia St, from 1st to Western Ave ■ (206) 682-7453 ■ www.pikeplace market.org

Open daily, except Christmas & Thanksgiving

Hmong Flower Stalls: www.pikeplacemarket.org/directory

Pike Place Fish Market: 86 Pike Place ■ (206) 682-7181

Starbucks: 1912 Pike Place ■ (206) 448-8762

Farmers Market: www.pikeplacemarket.org/farmers-market

First and Pike News: 93 Pike St ■ (206) 624-0140

DeLaurenti: 1435 1st Ave; 1-800-873-6685

■ **Three Girls Bakery (1514 Pike St)** offers fresh bread and sandwiches.

6 Buskers

Street music is a constant feature of market life. Visitors may catch the hyperkinetic show of a spoons player, who has featured in at least one award-winning rock video; or be entertained by gospel quartets, piano troubadours, or a clarinet soloist **(left)**.

RACHEL THE PIG

Be sure not to miss Rachel, Seattle's largest piggy bank. This brassy icon of the Market Foundation also serves as the market's sentry at the main entrance. All proceeds from visitors' donations to Rachel go toward low-income community groups.

Pike Place Market

8 Underground Mezzanines

Follow a maze of ramps and stairways to reach this shopping wonderland. Browse the books and collectibles, pay a visit to the palm reader, commission a portrait, or buy local arts and crafts as souvenirs.

9 Hillclimb

This enclosed stairway and elevator connects the market to the waterfront and more stores and restaurants in between. It also offers enchanting, far-reaching sea-to-mountain views.

7 Victor Steinbrueck Park

The wonderful grassy hill here makes this a popular lunch destination. Pack a picnic and drink in the gorgeous views of the Olympic Mountains, Puget Sound, and the city's skyline **(below)**.

4 Farmers Market

Sample the produce of Washington's organic farmers at the always popular outdoor Farmers Market, held on Tuesday through Friday from June through September. Stalls are located at various spots around downtown.

10 DeLaurenti

Step inside this Mediterranean gourmet grocery to sample some of its delicious offerings. Combine its fresh breads, cheeses, and large wine selection to create a great summer picnic.

5 First and Pike News

This quaint, old-fashioned newsstand offers a wide array of newspapers and magazines from around the world. The stand has been here since 1979.

TOP 10 ⭐ Seattle Center

The site of the 1962 Century 21 Exposition, "America's Space Age World's Fair," Seattle Center has thrived through decades of growth all around it. The main attraction is still the Space Needle, though a close second is the controversial Museum of Pop Culture, Paul Allen's monument to rock music. The International Fountain also attracts throngs of visitors. The center is the site of lavish presentations of art, theater, dance, and music all year long.

1 Seattle Children's Theatre (SCT)

Some 220,000 patrons are entertained by this organization **(above)** each year. The Charlotte Martin and Eve Alvord theaters are known for their family-orientated programs.

Seattle Center

2 McCaw Hall

The luxurious McCaw Hall *(see p42)* is home to the Seattle Opera and Pacific Northwest Ballet. The site also contains a café.

3 Chihuly Garden and Glass

Bright, organic shapes by internationally renowned glass sculptor Dale Chihuly sparkle in three distinct settings: museum installations, a glass house, and a garden **(right)**.

4 Museum of Pop Culture

Co-founder of Microsoft and avid rock enthusiast, Paul Allen commissioned the distinguished modern architect Frank Gehry to design this technicolor exhibition and performance space **(below)**. It is also home to the Science Fiction Hall of Fame *(see p40)*.

5 Bumbershoot

Seattleites mark their calendars for the long Labor Day holiday weekend in September, when Bumbershoot brings imaginative literary arts programs, artists, independent films, musicians, ethnic food, visual arts, and many other surprises to Seattle Center *(see p60)*.

8 Pacific Science Center

Visitors will find exhibits on topics such as electronic music-making, robotics, hydraulics, and natural history **(left)** highly entertaining and informative. There are two IMAX theaters and an area for toddlers.

1962 WORLD'S FAIR

The fair's designers demonstrated their vision of the future in 1962. Modernity ruled, from the science-fiction-esque Space Needle and monorail to the Sputnik-like Center Fountain. Nearly 10 million visitors came to marvel at this ideal future, and even Elvis Presley made an appearance, filming *It Happened at the World's Fair* (1963). Today, it is considered strictly retro, if not a little kitsch.

NEED TO KNOW

MAP H2 ■ (206) 684-7200 ■ www.seattle center.com

Space Needle: (206) 905-2100; open 9am–9pm Mon–Sat, 9am–8pm Sun; www.spaceneedle.com

McCaw Hall: (206) 733-9725; www.mccawhall. com

Museum of Pop Culture: (206) 770-2700; www. mopop.org

Seattle Center Monorail: (206) 905-2620; www. seattlemonorail.com

KeyArena: (206) 684-7200; www.keyarena. com

Pacific Science Center: 200 2nd Ave N; (206) 443-2001; www.pacific sciencecenter.org

Seattle Children's Theatre (SCT): 201 Thomas St; (206) 441-3322; www.sct.org

■ Head to Queen Anne Ave for dining options. For baked goods and coffee, try Uptown Espresso & Bakery (525 Queen Anne Ave N).

6 Seattle Center Monorail

Planners of the 1962 World's Fair imagined this as the future of mass transit *(see p41)*. The monorail makes the 1-mile (1.6-km) trip between here and downtown every ten minutes.

7 Center House

This large building houses the wonderful Seattle Children's Museum *(see p50)* as well as a theater, cafés, restaurants, and shops.

9 Space Needle

This imposing structure **(left)** is recognized as the city's architectural icon *(see p40)*. Ride the external elevators to the observation deck for a majestic view, or reserve a table at the revolving SkyCity restaurant for panoramic views.

10 KeyArena

The largest venue *(see p42)* in Seattle Center, with events ranging from music concerts to basketball games.

🔟 ⭐ Seattle Waterfront

One of Seattle's most distinguishing features is its waterfront. The core of the city's thriving maritime community, it is full of the sights, sounds, and smells of a seaport metropolis. It is the place to catch ferries to the Kitsap Peninsula or Bainbridge Island, or to visit the Seattle Aquarium. The piers are tourist hotspots, replete with restaurants and bars, shops, and harbor tours. Sculptures by well-known modern artists fill the nearby Olympic Sculpture Park.

Seattle Aquarium ①

The waterfront's most popular all-weather attraction is the world-class Seattle Aquarium. Make a point of stepping inside the aquarium's glass-domed room **(right)** under 400,000 gallons of water for spectacular views of sharks and octopuses.

SEATTLE MARITIME FESTIVAL AND THE TUGBOAT RACES

One of the most famed summer events is this festival that includes tugboat races on Elliott Bay. Not sleek but not sluggish, these boats are really something to behold (see p60).

② Cruise Ship Terminals

Seattle's proximity to Alaska's stunning Inside Passage, coupled with trends in leisure travel, led the city to build two terminals to accommodate the thousands of passengers. Watch ships docking at Bell Harbor Marina all summer long.

③ Ye Olde Curiosity Shop

Looking for literature etched on rice grains, or other unique objects? Since 1899, this has been the place to find curios, both from the distant and recent past. It also sells a selection of coastal Native American art.

7 Olympic Sculpture Park

At the southern end of Myrtle Edwards Park, this space has sculptures by Alexander Calder, Ellsworth Kelly, Jaume Plensa **(left)**, and others. The views from the park are sensational.

4 Washington State Ferries

An icon of the Pacific Northwest, these ferries provide a picturesque, inexpensive cruise across Puget Sound, as well as transporting Seattle's commuters *(see p110)*.

5 Watersports and Tours

Adventure-seekers can strap on a paraglider and head up for a breathtaking ride and aerial city view. Many boat cruises depart from here.

6 Bell Harbor Marina

This harbor **(below)** provides moorage for pleasure boats (large and small). It is adjacent to the cruise-ship terminal.

8 Tillicum Village, Blake Island

The four-hour visit to this Native American cultural center begins with a 45-minute narrated cruise. Visitors will be welcomed with steamed clams in broth, served salmon baked over an alder fire, and witness a spectacular show of traditional dance, songs, and stories.

9 Seattle Great Wheel

For spectacular views of the city skyline, a 20-minute spin on Seattle's Great Wheel *(see p71)* is a must. The 175-ft-(53-m-) tall structure, with 42 gondolas, is perched dramatically over Elliott Bay.

Seattle Waterfront

10 Myrtle Edwards Park

Visit this waterfront haven **(below)** for fine views of Mount Rainier, Puget Sound, and the Olympic Mountains. A bike trail and pedestrian path winds along the Elliott Bay coastline.

NEED TO KNOW

MAP H4–5

Seattle Aquarium: Pier 59; (206) 386-4300; open 9:30am–5pm daily; closed Thanksgiving & Christmas; adm; www.seattle aquarium.org

Ye Olde Curiosity Shop: Pier 54; (206) 682-5844; open summer: 9am–9:30pm; winter: 10am–6pm Sun–Thu, 9am–9pm Fri–Sat; www.yeolde curiosityshop.com

Washington State Ferries: Pier 52; (206) 464-6400; www.wsdot.wa.gov

Olympic Sculpure Park: 2901 Western Ave; (206) 654-3100

Tillicum Village, Blake Island: Pier 55; (206) 622-8687; see website for departure times; adm $84 adults, $75 seniors, $32 5–12 years (under-5s free); www.argosycruises.com

Seattle Great Wheel: (206) 623-8600; open summer: 10am–11pm Sun–Thu, 10am–midnight Fri–Sat (winter hours may vary); adm; www.seattlegreat wheel.com

Pioneer Square

The birthplace of modern Seattle has a colorful history marked by economic and geological fluctuations. The Great Fire of 1889 virtually destroyed it, before Alaska's Gold Rush breathed new life and Victorian architecture into the mix. The old warehouses gave rise to a thriving loft scene in the 1980s and 1990s. While rents have skyrocketed and developers continue to renovate the grand facades of relic buildings, the galleries, cafés, and entrepreneurial spirit remain. Much has been restored after the devastating 2001 Nisqually earthquake.

④ Pioneer Square

This cobblestone triangle of recreational land, bordered by Yesler Way and First Avenue, is notable for its Tlingit totem pole, and its statue of Seattle's namesake, Chief Sealth (see p37). The square also features an iron-and-glass pergola **(left)** built in 1909, which once marked the entrance to the "finest underground restroom in the United States". Historic street lamps complete the old-world feel of the park.

① First Thursdays

On the first Thursday of each month, from noon to 8pm, galleries sponsor an art walk. Patrons can talk directly to the artists about their work. Start the tour on Occidental Way (see p58).

③ Skid Road

Henry Yesler's logging mill – used for sliding timber down to the wharf – sat at the foot of what is now Yesler Way. When Pioneer Square's economy tumbled, Skid Road came to signify desolation.

② Seattle Metropolitan Police Museum

Police artifacts dating from the 1880s – including weapons, uniforms, and photographs – are on display at this intriguing museum. Visitors can learn about some of Seattle's most notorious crime cases.

⑤ Merchants Cafe and Saloon

Popular and prospering since 1890, Seattle's oldest restaurant and bar dishes up hearty meals amid its little-changed Victorian decor **(below)**.

NEED TO KNOW

MAP K5

Seattle Metropolitan Police Museum: 317 3rd Ave S; (206) 748-9991; www.seametropolice museum.org; open 11am–4pm Tue–Sun; adm $4 adults, $2 under-12s

Merchant's Café and Saloon: 109 Yesler Way; (206) 467-5070

Bill Speidel's Underground Tour: 614 1st Ave; (206)

682-4646; www.under groundtour.com

Smith Tower: 506 2nd Ave; adm for observation deck; www.smithtower.com

King Street Station: 303 S Jackson St; open 24 hours daily

Klondike Gold Rush National Historical Park: 319 2nd Ave S; (206) 220-4240

Waterfall Garden Park: 219 2nd Ave South; open 8am–3:45pm Mon–Fri

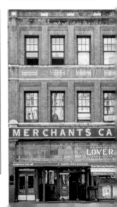

7 Smith Tower

Built in 1914 by typewriter tycoon L. C. Smith, this sky-scraper **(left)**, at 38 stories, was once the tallest edifice west of New York. Renovated in 2015, it has an open-air observation deck with a bar and sweeping views *(see p41)*.

8 King Street Station

This beautifully restored train station is a gateway to Seattle. Its upper floors are being transformed into spaces for art and cultural events.

NISQUALLY EARTHQUAKE

In February 2001, the entire Puget Sound region experienced a 40-second earthquake, measuring 6.8 on the Richter scale. Several otherwise sturdy and fireproof brick-and-mortar constructions from post-1889 met their match *(see p37)*.

Pioneer Square

10 Klondike Gold Rush National Historical Park

A versatile display of exhibits, films, and photographs charts Seattle's role as the closest US city to the Alaskan gold rush, and its role as a crucial supply post for claim-stakers *(see p36)*.

6 Bill Speidel's Underground Tour

Deliberately unusual in name and nature, this tour presents a remarkable look at the area's underground history. The Great Fire, tidal patterns, and poor sewage design forced citizens to convert second stories into first, shown through this subterranean 90-minute walk starting from the Pioneer Building *(see p41)*.

9 Waterfall Garden

In the Northwest, water is everywhere. Step inside this tiny private park to relax and meditate by this 22 ft (7 m) man-made waterfall **(below)**.

🔟⭐ International District

Once known as Chinatown, this district was renamed when some community leaders recognized that inhabitants from all over Asia had made that term obsolete. One of Seattle's most historic districts, "the ID" is a striking example of how Asian cultures have thrived in Western society. Each ethnicity claims an area, even while coexisting in the same vibrant part of town. Stroll through groceries and restaurants run by Koreans, Japanese, Vietnamese, and others, to experience Asia, Pacific Northwest style.

1 Wing Luke Museum

The vision of civic leader Wing Luke, who died in a plane crash in 1965, this interesting museum (below) explores the culture, history, and influence of Asian Pacific Americans through a series of permanent and visiting exhibitions (see p39).

2 Tsue Chong Co. Inc.

Any sweet smells amid the strong aromas of the International District are likely to be coming from this factory store, which makes delicious noodles and fortune cookies.

3 Dim Sum

Seattleites are famously serious about their food, and the International District is well-known for these mandatory steamed Chinese delicacies. The best places can be found around S King St and S Jackson St, and are cheap and cheerful.

5 Panama Hotel Tea House

This historic building, adjacent to the Panama Hotel (see p119), was once a bath-house. Now it is a tea-room serving the finest teas from around the world.

4 Seattle's Best Tea

Tea finds its rightful place in a city overrun by coffee shops. Joe Hsu's small, bright, modern shop is the place to go to sample from a large range of teas. Prices range from $20 to over $200 per pound (left).

6 Uwajimaya

Those who cannot make it to the Far East should head to the biggest Asian market in the Pacific Northwest. This store has a vast array of Asian merchandise, and a huge ethnic food court.

Previous pages Alki Point Lighthouse, seen from Alki Beach Park

⑧ Union Station

Opened in 1911, this Beaux Arts-style former train station **(left)** boasts a black-and-white mosaic floor and a 55-ft (16-m) vaulted ceiling that supports hundreds of lights. It was sensationally remodeled in 2000, and is now popular as an events venue.

CHINESE LUNAR NEW YEAR

A traditional celebration in Chinese communities worldwide, Seattle's version takes place inside the historic Union Station. Kung Fu lion dances, music, and firework displays make for a festive day.

⑨ Safeco Field and CenturyLink Field

Seattle's professional baseball and soccer teams are based just across the street from each other, in between International District and Pioneer Square.

International District

Kung Fu lion dance, Chinese Lunar New Year

⑦ Great Wall Mall

This 9-acre (3.6-ha) mall offers an amazing Asian shopping extravaganza. It is a fair drive to the east of Sea-Tac Airport, but the sheer size and selection of these Asian import stores is worth seeing.

⑩ Little Saigon

The storefronts here resemble images of 1960s-era Saigon, with large, bright signage in Vietnamese.

NEED TO KNOW

MAP L6 ■ (206) 382-1197 ■ www.cidbia.org

Wing Luke Museum: 719 S King St; (206) 623-5124; open 10am–5pm Tue–Sun (to 8pm on 1st Thu of month); adm; www.wingluke.org

Seattle's Best Tea: 506 S King St; (206) 749-9855

Uwajimaya: 600 5th Ave S; (206) 624-6248

Great Wall Mall: 18230 E Valley Hwy, Kent; (425) 251-1600; open 9am–9pm daily

Union Station: 401 S Jackson St; (206) 398-5000

Tsue Chong Co. Inc.: 800 Weller St S; (206) 623-0801; open 9:30am–5pm Mon–Fri, 10:30am–2pm Sat

Safeco Field: (206) 346-4000

CenturyLink Field: (206) 381-7555

■ If you want authentic dim sum, try Jade Garden (424 7th Ave S; 622-8181), Harbor City Restaurant (707 S King St; 621-2228), or Dim Sum King (617 S Jackson St; 682-2823).

Broadway

This is the main drag that slices across Capitol Hill, one of Seattle's edgier communities just up the hill from downtown. Hip stores and a variety of restaurants and cafés attract a thriving gay culture and gritty youth population. On warm nights, Broadway is about as urban as Seattle gets, surging with pedestrians. Thanks to the avenue's proclivity for over-the-edge fashion, people-watching can be a great source of entertainment. Sleek new condos and retail spaces, and a light-rail station are changing the face of Broadway.

Unicorn ①
This bar is part carnival arcade, part circus, part wildlife museum, and 100 percent camp (right). Drag shows are performed on weekends and are strictly for those over 21.

NEED TO KNOW

MAP L3–M3

Unicorn: 1118 E Pike St; (206) 325-6492; www.unicornseattle.com

Broadway Performance Hall: 1625 Broadway; (206) 325-3113

The Elliott Bay Book Company: 1521 10th Ave; (206) 624-6600; www.elliottbaybook.com

Dick's Drive-In: 115 Broadway Ave E; (206) 323-1300

The Vajra: 518 Broadway Ave E; (206) 323-7846

Red Light: 312 Broadway Ave E; (206) 329-2200; www.redlightvintage.com

Cal Anderson Park: 11th between Pine St E/Denny Way E

■ There are several pockets of panhandlers and homeless street people along Broadway. Use your discretion if asked for donations.

② Broadway Performance Hall
Originally Broadway High School, the hall *(see p43)* forms part of the campus for Seattle Central Community College. Seattle architect Victor Steinbrueck was an instrumental figure in restoring this structure. Its repertoire includes film festivals and music and dance recitals.

The Elliott Bay Book Company ③
This destination store (right) offers more than 150,000 books, frequent author talks and events, and – of course – a café.

④ Dick's Drive-In
Open since 1954, this is Seattle's very own version of a fast-food hamburger joint. This branch is a magnet for crowds on weekend nights. The food is delicious, but not great for cholesterol-watchers.

7 Dance Steps on Broadway

Sculptor Jack Mackie created an amusing series of inlaid bronze dance steps along the sidewalks of Broadway in 1982. Each one features the instructions of a dance style, such as the rumba **(left)**, the tango, and the foxtrot.

PILL HILL

This is an affectionate term for First Hill, the area almost indistinct from Capitol Hill along the same high ridge above downtown. It is thick with most of the area's medical research facilities and hospitals, hence the nickname.

9 Jimi Hendrix Statue

This bronze sculpture *(see p80)* of rock legend Jimi Hendrix is located by the popular Pike/Pine corridor.

Broadway

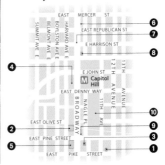

5 Egyptian Theatre

Broadway's vintage movie house *(see p43)* showcases independent films from directors on the vanguard. The Seattle International Film Festival *(see p60)* makes liberal use of the theater each year.

6 The Vajra

The name roughly translates as "Destroyer of Ignorance", and this store sells a selection of Tibetan Buddhist meditation supplies. Look for block-print tapestries, scented oils, and incense. It is also a popular spot for tarot-card reading.

8 Red Light

A two-story bastion of quirk and fashion, this is Seattle's largest store stocking vintage apparel. Choose from the extensive and varied collection with help from the friendly and well-informed staff.

10 Cal Anderson Park

Named after one of Washington's openly gay legislators, the park features Lincoln Reservoir, Bobby Morris Playfield, tennis courts, a play area, and an interactive water feature **(below)**.

TOP10 ⭐ Lake Washington Ship Canal

What began in Montlake as a tiny log flume is now an 8-mile (13-km) urban waterway for sailboats, kayakers, and an impressive fleet of industrial vessels heading to sea. In 1854, pioneer Thomas Mercer recognized the need for a passage to the ocean from Lake Union and Lake Washington, and the Ship Canal and locks were finished in 1917 by the US Army Corps of Engineers. Four bridges cross the canal in Ballard, Fremont, the University District, and Montlake.

1 Montlake
At the base of Capitol Hill's northeastern tip, the upscale community of Montlake abuts the arboretum and the Ship Canal. Just across the canal, the university's huge Husky Stadium (see p28) dominates the view. The annual Opening Day Boat Parade attracts large crowds to the canal (**above**).

2 Working Waterfront
The maritime industry prospers along the canal. Tankers lie in dry dock, boat dealers proliferate, and oil booms float about while the natural ecology struggles to survive.

3 Making the Cut
Seattle district engineer for the Army Corps of Engineers, Hiram M. Chittenden lobbied Congress to fund the project in 1911, and Lake Washington was leveled to accomodate boat traffic.

NEED TO KNOW
MAP E2

Visitor Center: 3015 NW 54th Street; open May–Sep: 10am–6pm daily, Oct–Apr: 10am–4pm Thu–Mon

Grounds: open 7am–9pm daily

Ballard Locks: 3015 NW 54th St; (206) 783-7059

■ Those planning on kayaking should be wary of weather changes any time of year, because winds can severely affect the current and water conditions.

Lake Washington Ship Canal

OPENING DAY EVENTS

Seattleites take water and boating seriously, but anyone can sail the waterways. The official boating season begins the first Saturday in May, with a series of waterborne celebrations sponsored by the smart Seattle Yacht Club. The constant drawbridge openings snarl traffic for the parade and regatta, as small ships fill the Ship Canal and adjacent lakes with revelers.

4 Lake Union

This is an urban lake with Seattle's downtown skyline framing its southern shore **(below)**. Visit Seattle's maritime museum, Center for Wooden Boats *(see p38)*, and Lake Union Park at the south end.

7 Bascule Bridges

These bridges operate with cantilevered sections that can be raised and lowered. Fremont and Ballard bridges are the oldest, built in 1917. The former is only 30 ft (9 m) above the waterline.

9 Urban Wildlife

Although the Ship Canal is literally and figuratively far from any wilderness, it attracts diverse wildlife. Blue heron, gulls, beaver, Canada geese, and migrating salmon are creatures to look out for.

5 Christmas Ships

Every December, local boaters celebrate the holiday season by venturing out during several cold evenings after decorating their boats with colorful light displays.

8 Shilshole Bay

The western end of the Ship Canal feeds into this scenic bay, home to a public marina. The waterfront boasts meeting spaces, fine seafood restaurants, and Golden Gardens park *(see p47)*.

6 Ballard Locks

Officially called the Hiram M. Chittenden Locks, these locks link the Sound and Salmon Bays at Ballard **(below)**. About 100,000 vessels pass through annually, as do salmon runs in the adjacent fish ladder – fully equipped with observation windows.

10 Sleepless in Seattle

The idiosyncratic floating home enclaves **(above)** of northern Lake Union and Portage Bay are visible almost exclusively by boats traveling the canal and its environs. One was a focal point in the Meg Ryan and Tom Hanks romantic film, *Sleepless in Seattle* (1993).

TOP 10 ⭐ University of Washington

Founded in November 1861, just ten years after the creation of Washington Territory, the prestigious UW moved to its present location with 639 hilly acres (258 ha) in 1895. Supporting a student body that is as eclectic as the architectural mix on campus, the institution has garnered an international reputation. The wide-open quads, cherry blossoms in spring, and lovely views provide a relaxing counterpoint to the buzz of advanced learning.

University campus

① Henry Art Gallery
Founded in 1927, this was the first public art gallery **(above)** in the state, which quadrupled its size in 1997 to make room for larger, modern exhibits and collections. It also has a bookstore and a café (see p38).

② Suzzallo Library
Once known as "the soul of the University," the library is the crowning glory of the Neo-Gothic style on campus. The astounding vaulted ceiling rises 65 ft (20 m) above the second floor reading room **(below)**.

③ Husky Stadium
Located at Capitol Hill's northeastern tip, the upscale Montlake abuts the arboretum and the Ship Canal (see pp26–7). Just across the canal sits the university's huge Husky Stadium, home of the UW Huskies.

④ Meany Center
The shining glory of professional performance arts on campus, the theater hosts performers of all disciplines from all over the globe. It also supports all of the school's drama, music, dance, and experimental digital media curricula.

⑤ Cherry Blossoms
Photographers, tourists, and painters flock to the Quad in early spring to witness an annual spectacle – the Yoshino cherry trees in full bloom. These stunning trees were donated by the mayor of Tokyo in 1912, marking a friendly alliance between the US and Japan.

⑥ University Book Store
The main branch of the bookstore rivals the best of the independent and larger chain book vendors for sheer selection and well-informed staff.

University of Washington

THE AVE

The main commercial artery serving the U District is University Way NE, called "The Ave". It is lined with coffee shops, clothiers, music stores, bookstores that have lasted generations, and restaurants serving reasonably priced food.

10 Medicinal Herb Garden

Escape for a captivating spell through 2.5 acres (1 ha) of land **(below)** where several hundred species flourish and herbal scents abound.

NEED TO KNOW

MAP E2–F2 ▪ (206) 543-9198 ▪ www. washington.edu

Henry Art Gallery: NE 41st St & 15th Ave NE; open 11am–4pm Wed–Fri & Sat–Sun, 11am–9pm Thu; adm; www.henryart.org

Husky Stadium: 3800 Montlake Blvd

Meany Center: 4001 University Way NE; (206) 543-4880; www. meany.org

Cherry Blossoms: uwtv.org/uw-quad-cherry-blossom-cam

University Book Store: 4326 University Way NE; (206) 634-3400

7 Paul G. Allen Center for Computer Science & Engineering

This $72-million state-of-the-art facility was named after one of the two founders of Microsoft **(below)**.

8 The Hub

The main student union building is known as "The Hub" due to its central position on campus. It is information central, as well as a venue for performers.

9 Red Square

Taking its name from the inlaid brick paving stones underfoot, the huge square lies between the Meany Center, Kane Hall, and the Suzzallo Library. It is also known for hosting impromptu midnight concerts.

📟🌟 Woodland Park Zoo

Designed in 1909 by landscape architect John Olmsted, this is one of the oldest zoos on the West Coast. Occupying an area of 92 acres (37 ha), the park offers a natural habitat for nearly 300 animal species. Reflecting a naturalistic mission to advocate conservation and education while imparting the great value of an ecological perspective, the animal habitats here are designed to be as close to nature as possible. African mammals roam a grassy savanna; African and Asian elephants thrive in a Thai-style setting; grizzly bears frolic over logs and in a stream running down a steep hill. Popular with young families is the petting zoo, a hands-on area that is both fun and educational.

African Savanna ①
Lions, giraffes, hippos, wild dogs, zebras, spotted hyenas, gazelles, patas monkeys, white-faced whistling ducks, and Egyptian geese make this city-bound safari one of the largest and most exhilarating places **(right)**. Observe the scene from the overlook dedicated to guitarist and Seattle native Jimi Hendrix.

② Gorillas
In one of the most cherished spots at the zoo, visitors can view two multigenerational gorilla families while they cavort only inches away on the other side of the thickened glass.

③ Northern Trail
Find the deceptively playful-looking grizzly bears here **(left)**. Nearby, the packs of gray or timber wolves seem haunted, and the extremely threatened river otters dive under-water and resurface with total abandon.

④ Butterfly Garden
During the warm months, this spot hosts as many as 500 butterflies from 15 different species. Visit the Pollinator Patio during the cold months and watch endangered butterflies as they hatch.

⑤ Komodo Dragons

These are the world's largest carnivorous lizards, weighing in at as much as 500 lb (226 kg) and spanning a length of up to 9 ft (3 m). The excellent swimmers are not recommended as pets, but they are great for the imagination.

⑦ Jaguar

The largest cat species in the Western Hemisphere, these mammals are an endangered species (above). Their habitat here features a cave, a pool for swimming, and jungle-like terrain that brings the fearsome animals close enough to touch, if not for the glass-surrounded enclosure.

⑧ Birds of Prey

Watch falconers send these regal winged predators out and back several times a day by the Raptor Center (left). Perched on fence posts, spectacled owls and ferruginous hawks sit calmly in full panoramic view.

⑥ Plants and Pathways

Take the time to appreciate the consideration that the zoo landscapers have given to this human environment. The shrubbery is lush and plentiful, and lends an exotic ambience to the place.

ZOOTUNES SUMMER CONCERTS

The zoo departs from its main agenda every summer with one of Seattle's top musical highlights. Residents from the surrounding neighborhood and all over town meet on the North Meadow in the late afternoons and early evenings for a picnic dinner, and take in entertainment from some of the best-known musicians worldwide.

⑨ Nocturnals

Take a break from the screech and howls of outdoor wildlife for the dark and silent mysteries of nocturnal creatures. Watch boas, pythons, vampire bats, tomato frogs, blue-tongued skinks, and much more.

⑩ Orangutans and Siamangs

With intelligence that approaches our own, orangutans are hilarious to observe (above). Also view siamangs, native to the island of Sumatra and the Malay Peninsula.

NEED TO KNOW

MAP D1 ▪ 601 North 59th St ▪ (206) 548-2500 ▪ www.zoo.org

Open May–Sep: 9:30am–6pm daily; Oct–Apr: 9:30am–4pm daily

Adm: Adults $20.95 May–Sep, $14.95 Oct–Apr; children (3–12) $12.95 May–Sep, $9.95 Oct–Apr

▪ Inside the West Gate are several places to eat in the Pavilion, where the Market Grill, Sabino's Specialties, Wok in the Wild, and other food counters are found.

▪ Be sure to visit the vast Woodland Park and Green Lake just the other side of Hwy 99 (Aurora Avenue) from the zoo.

🔟 ⭐ Discovery Park

Occupying the northwestern edge of the Magnolia headland north of Elliott Bay, Discovery Park is Seattle's largest and most varied in-city escape. Even though the US Army's Fort Lawton sold surplus base territory to the city, Army Reserves still use a part of the park for training and officers' quarters. At a vast 534 acres (216 ha), Discovery Park consists of densely wooded rainforests crisscrossed with trails, high bluffs of eroding sand at the edge of a huge meadow, and 2 miles (3 km) of driftwood-laden beaches on Puget Sound.

NEED TO KNOW

MAP A2 ■ (206) 684-4075 ■ www.seattle.gov/parks

Open 4am–11:30pm daily

Visitors' Center: 3801 Discovery Park Blvd; (206) 386-4236; open 8:30am–5pm Tue–Sun

Daybreak Star Indian Cultural Center: (206) 285-4425; www.unitedindians.org

■ Plan an itinerary based on the time you have. There are no concessions in the park, so bring a picnic lunch.

① Eagle-Watching

Occasionally, bald eagles nest in the highest treetops in Discovery Park, home to more than 250 species of birds and other wildlife. You may find park volunteers surrounded by eager bird-watchers with binoculars. Chances are they have sighted a nest.

② Daybreak Star Indian Cultural Center

Operated by the United Indians of All Tribes Foundation, this cultural center houses an interesting collection of Native American art. There is also an arts and crafts gallery, traditional salmon bakes, and an annual summer powwow celebration on the Discovery Park grounds.

Discovery Park

4 Playgrounds

For an outing with children, head for the small playground behind park headquarters at the east entrance **(left)**. Or, ask for one of only five parking passes available for families with young children in order to be able to drive directly down to the alluring shore of Puget Sound.

5 Military Residences

The park is dotted with abandoned and still-in-use army base housing, listed on the National Register of Historic Places. Most are off-limits, but get a closer look at them near the former parade grounds.

6 Beach Walks at Low Tide

Seattleites escaping the city come to walk along the waterfront parks around the Sound. The beach at Discovery Park is a preferred spot for those in the know **(left)**.

3 West Point Treatment Plant

A reminder of the city outside, this facility is so exquisitely landscaped as to be almost invisible from hiking trails. This ultramodern wastewater treatment plant is about as environmentally conscious as today's technology allows.

7 West Point Lighthouse

As picturesque as can be, the lighthouse shines light through the rolling fog from its high perch on a narrow spit of land jutting out into the water **(below)**. Feel free to stroll up to and around the automated sentinel, even though it is not open for touring.

SHARING THE LAND

Land use at Discovery Park represents the harmonious balance between conservation and urban develop-ment. In 1970, activist Bernie Whitebear staged an occupation of the still-active military base, in part to establish a cultural land foundation for urban Indians. After an exhausting three months, Whitebear's group acquired a 99-year parkland lease.

8 Bluff Trail

The trail **(below)** leads from the South Gate along a meadow's edge to the overlook, with views of Puget Sound and the Olympic Mountains.

9 Loop Trail

Stroll along this trail through the varied terrain of Discovery Park. Explore the easy route to find overgrown rainforest ravines, flowering mead-owlands, creeks, sand dunes, thickets, and brambles galore.

10 Go Fly a Kite

The hilly field between the main bluffs and a radar ball behind barbed wire makes for some of the best kite fly-ing around, as the sea updrafts seem constant.

The Top 10 of Everything

Detail of Frank Gehry's visionary
exterior of the Museum of Pop Culture

🔟 Moments in History

Illustration showing 18th-century lumber merchants on Puget Sound

1 Native American Roots

Archaeological records date the first inhabitants of the Seattle region to 11,000–12,000 years ago. Early settlers included the Nisqually, Suquamish, Duwamish, Snoqualmie, and Muckleshoot tribes.

Snoqualmie Indians harvesting crops

2 Denny Party

In 1851, Chief Sealth of the Duwamish Tribe greeted Arthur A. Denny and his group of European settlers at West Seattle's Alki Point (see p104). Subsequently, Denny served as a delegate to the Monticello convention, which gave rise to the states of Oregon and Washington.

3 Northern Pacific Railroad

Seattle's neighboring city, Tacoma, was the original terminus of 1873's Northern Pacific Railroad, linking the region to the rest of the country. By 1893, another transcontinental railroad, the Great Northern Railway, extended into Seattle, eventually supplanting Tacoma as the Puget Sound region's main rail depot.

4 Lumber Mills

When timber baron Frederick Weyerhaeuser purchased nearly 1,550 sq miles (4,000 sq km) of railroad land in 1900, Seattle's mush-rooming logging industry turned a corner for even more rapid growth and exploitation of natural resources. Until then, entrepreneurs such as Henry Yesler ruled the wharf, and erected the pioneer town out of lumber from ancient old growth forests.

5 Great Fire of 1889

Natural resources created a boomtown whose rapid growth drew more than 1,000 new residents every month. Seattleites learned the fragility of wooden structures in 1889, after a catastrophic fire destroyed much of the downtown area.

6 Klondike Gold Rush

The Alaska Gold Rush (see p19) officially kicked off in 1897 after a gold-filled steamship docked at Seattle's waterfront. As the last stop for prospectors and suppliers bound for the gold fields, the city prospered.

7 Boeing's Beginnings

Recognizing the need for airplanes as the US entered World War I in 1917, William E. Boeing hired pilot Herb Munter to design a seaplane for the Navy. Boeing is now the world's largest aerospace company.

8 Rise of Microsoft

In 1975, Harvard dropout Bill Gates and his high-school friend Paul Allen founded Microsoft. From the Seattle suburb of Redmond, they launched a personal computer revolution and have never looked back. Today, Microsoft's Windows operating system is the dominant computer platform, and the company employs more than 114,000 people worldwide.

Microsoft's Bill Gates and Paul Allen

9 Nisqually Earthquake

Seattle suffered from a major magnitude-6.8 earthquake on the morning of February 28, 2001 *(see p19)*. Workers escaped their offices, if they could, to see the earth rolling, pavements cracking, and cars violently swaying. The region suffered more than $1 billion in damages.

10 Green River Killer Caught

The Seattle area lived under a dark shadow of brutal serial killings as dozens of women became victims of the Green River Killer. Twenty years of intense investigation led to the capture of Gary Ridgway in 2001.

TOP 10 FAMOUS SEATTLEITES

Kung fu legend Bruce Lee

1 Chief Sealth (1786–1866)
Seattle draws its name from the Suquamish and Duwamish leader.

2 John W. Nordstrom (1871–1963)
Originally shoe sellers, the Nordstrom family empire is now a national chain of upscale department stores.

3 Nellie Centennial Cornish (1876–1956)
A great pioneer of the Seattle art scene, she founded the Cornish College of the Arts in 1914.

4 Cecile Anne Hansen (b. 1934)
The chairwoman of the Duwamish tribe and descendant of Chief Sealth is an advocate for the recognition of Seattle's first people.

5 Bruce Lee (1940–1973)
This kung fu legend and movie star lived in Seattle and is buried here.

6 Jimi Hendrix (1942–1970)
A self-taught guitarist and legend, Hendrix continues to influence today's music with his original compositions.

7 Nancy Pearl (b. 1945)
The celebrity librarian was author of *Book Lust*, and is an ambassador for a city full of readers.

8 Gary Locke (b. 1950)
The first Chinese-American governor in US history, Locke was also Secretary of Commerce from 2009 to 2011.

9 Bill Gates (b. 1955)
Co-founder and now technology advisor of Microsoft, he is one of the world's richest men.

10 Jeff Bezos (b. 1964)
This internet billionaire founded giant web retailer Amazon in 1995.

🔟 Museums

① Henry Art Gallery

This modern art museum *(see pp28–29)* at UW presents work by cutting-edge artists. It also offers numerous imaginative programs and exhibits, and promotes experimental art by encouraging dialogue on contemporary culture and aesthetics.

Temporary exhibit, Henry Art Gallery

② Seattle Asian Art Museum

MAP E4 ■ 1400 E Prospect St ■ (206) 654-3100 ■ Open 10am–5pm Wed–Sun (to 9pm Thu) ■ Adm (free 1st Thu of month) ■ www.seattle artmuseum.org

The historic 1933 Art-Moderne structure in Volunteer Park houses Seattle Art Museum's Asian art collection. The museum is currently closed for renovation until 2019.

③ Frye Art Museum

MAP L4 ■ 704 Terry Ave ■ (206) 622-9250 ■ Open 11am–5pm Tue–Sun (to 7pm Thu) ■ Adm ■ www.fryemuseum.org

Wealthy industrialists Emma and Charles Frye's collection of 19th- to 20th-century representational art is on view at this elegant gallery. Exhibits include works by American masters such as Mary Cassatt, John Singer Sargent, and Andrew Wyeth.

④ Living Computers

MAP D6 ■ 2245 1st Ave South ■ (206) 342-2020 ■ Open 10am–5pm Wed–Sun (to 8pm 1st Thu of month) ■ Adm (free 5–8pm 1st Thu of month) ■ www.livingcomputers.org

In 2006, Microsoft co-founder Paul Allen founded this museum which exhibits the world's largest collection of vintage operating computers. The museum opened to the public in 2012 and offers experiences with robotics, virtual reality, artificial intelligence, self-driving cars, video-game making, and digital art.

⑤ Center for Wooden Boats

MAP K1 ■ 1010 Valley St ■ (206) 382-2628 ■ Open 10am–8pm Tue–Sun (to 5pm in winter) ■ www.cwb.org

CWB has over 100 small vessels and offers classes in maritime activities and crafts. During its annual July festival, relic sloops and tugs can be toured. For an in-city adventure, try sailing one of the historic boats.

⑥ Seattle Art Museum

The tall, black metal *Hammering Man* by Jonathan Borofsky stands outside Seattle's largest art museum *(see p72)*. SAM's permanent collection includes Asian, European, African, and Native American works.

European Gallery, Seattle Art Museum

Museum of History & Industry exhibit

(7) Museum of History & Industry

MAP K1 ▪ 860 Terry Ave N ▪ (206) 324-1126 ▪ Open 10am–5pm daily (to 8pm Thu) ▪ Adm (free 1st Thu of month) ▪ www.mohai.org

Located in Lake Union Park, this is a gem for anyone interested in the region's work and workforce over the last 150 years. Key features of this museum include photographs and a rich library of oral histories.

(8) Museum of Flight

MAP P2 ▪ 9404 E Marginal Way S ▪ (206) 764-5720 ▪ Open 10am–5pm daily (to 9pm 1st Thu of month) ▪ Adm ▪ www.museumofflight.org

Walk through a model of the Space Shuttle, tour the first Air Force One, designed for President Kennedy, climb into the cockpit of a SR-71 Blackbird or F/A-18 Hornet jet, or step aboard Concorde (see p50).

(9) Northwest African American Museum

MAP F6 ▪ 2300 S Massachusetts St ▪ (206) 518-6000 ▪ Open 11am–5pm Wed–Sun (to 7pm Thu) ▪ Adm (free 1st Thu of month) ▪ www.naamnw.org

Here visitors can trace the history and traditions of African-Americans in the Pacific Northwest, from slavery to the present day.

(10) Wing Luke Museum

Named after a civic leader who lobbied for Asian-American rights, this museum fulfills Wing's dream to showcase the culture and history of Asian immigrants (see p22).

TOP 10 NORTHWEST ARTISTS

1 Mark Tobey (1890–1976)
A 1953 *Life* magazine featured Tobey as one of the four "Mystic Painters of the Pacific Northwest." He was a major influence on Jackson Pollock.

2 Kenneth Callahan (1905–1986)
Another artist in the aforementioned *Life* feature, Callahan was once a curator at Seattle Art Museum.

3 Paul Horiuchi (1906–1999)
Japan-born Horiuchi used heavily textured, Abstract Expressionist collage painting utilizing Zen philosophy to create his mysterious works.

4 George Tsutakawa (1910–1997)
He gained international fame as a painter, sculptor, and fountain-maker.

5 Morris Graves (1910–2001)
This Northwest painter continues to inspire Seattle artists.

6 Jacob Lawrence (1917–2000)
Lawrence established a national reputation as a painter and activist.

7 Fay Jones (b. 1936)
The monumental painter behind the Pop Art Westlake tunnel mural, Jones's work can be seen at SAM.

8 Dale Chihuly (b. 1941)
Chihuly's handblown decorative glass art has popularized the medium.

9 Barbara Earl Thomas (b. 1948)
The first director of the Northwest African American Museum is a recipient of the local "Genius" award.

10 Deborah Moore (b. 1960)
Once a member of Dale Chihuly's team, this glass artist is best-known for her monumental glass orchids.

Portrait of Jacob Lawrence

Architectural Highlights

Colored sheet-metal exterior of the Museum of Pop Culture

1 Museum of Pop Culture

Designed by the renowned Post-Modern architect, Frank Gehry, this technicolor edifice *(see pp14–15)* resembles a smashed guitar, in provocative homage to Seattle-born Jimi Hendrix's incendiary finales. Microsoft co-founder Paul Allen's project emphasizes Seattle's role in the artistic and musical movement.

2 Central Library

Award-winning Dutch architect Rem Koolhaas designed this $196 million insulated glass-and-steel structure to replace Seattle's vintage 1960 Central Library. The unusual oblique structure and glass flooring have been controversial, but defenders of the building insist that, once inside, people will love it *(see p72)*.

3 Columbia Center

This 76-story skyscraper rises high above any other Seattle structure. Completed in 1985, from a design by Chester Lindsey Architects, it is currently the second-tallest building west of the Mississippi River. Three of the 46 elevators bring visitors to the posh private club at the top. There is also an observation deck on the 73rd floor that offers stunning panoramic views across Elliott Bay, the Olympic Peninsula, Mount Rainier, and beyond to the Cascade Mountains *(see p73)*.

4 Amazon Biosphere

MAP J3 ■ **2117–2127 7th Ave**

Online retail giant Amazon conceived this complex as a greenhouse-like social center. The three conjoined globes resemble water molecules and the scaffolding is visible through the greenish glass skin. Entry is for Amazon employees only; city visitors will have to make do with studying the building from the outside.

5 Space Needle

Seattle's modern architectural identity began with the Space Needle *(see p15)*, designed by architect firm John Graham & Company, for the 1962 World's Fair. The three pairs of beams supporting the spire lie buried 30 ft (8 m) underground, and have secured the 605-ft (185-m) Needle during several earth-quakes and gale-force windstorms.

Iconic Space Needle

6 Rainier Tower
MAP K4 ■ 1301 5th Ave

Designed by renowned architect Minoru Yamasaki in 1977, this unique 40-story structure resembles an upside-down skyscraper, as its main tower rises from a relatively narrow 11-story pedestal. Rainier Square, an upscale underground mall, is located beneath the tower.

7 Smith Tower

Typewriter tycoon L. C. Smith erected Seattle's first skyscraper (see pp18–19) in 1914. The white terracotta building has brass hand-operated elevators that take visitors to the Chinese Room at the 35th level, with its antique carvings, inlaid porcelain ceiling, and an observation deck.

8 Seattle Tower
MAP K4 ■ 1218 3rd Ave

This charming Art Deco building was designed by architects Albertson, Wilson & Richardson in 1929. The facade's tan brick and multiple shades of granite set it apart from its steel-and-glass neighbors. Vertical accents make its 27 stories appear even taller, and the lobby's ornate bronze and marble detail is capped by a decorative ceiling bas-relief.

9 Seattle Center Monorail

One of the city's favorite attractions is taking an exciting two-minute ride on the monorail (see p15) designed by Alweg Rapid Transit Systems. Each year, 1.5 million passengers board its original 1962 cars to get a taste of what designers imagined at the time would be the mass transit model of the future. The monorail connects the downtown area with the Seattle Center, and departures take place every ten minutes from Westlake Center (5th & Pine Sts) and the Seattle Center.

Pioneer Building facade

10 Pioneer Building
MAP K5 ■ 608 1st Ave

This striking 1892 building of red brick and terracotta, designed by Elmer H. Fisher, was the city's tallest building until 1904, and boasts a National Historic Landmark status. During the Gold Rush years (see p36), 48 mining outfits maintained offices here, and it became headquarters for a prosperous speakeasy during Prohibition. Bill Speidel's Underground Tour (see pp18–19) starts here.

TOP 10 Performing Arts Venues

Glitzy foyer of the Paramount Theatre

Seattle Repertory Theatre
MAP H1 ■ 155 Mercer St ■ (877) 900-9285 ■ www.seattlerep.org

The Bagley Wright Hall at the Seattle Center belongs to the nonprofit Seattle Repertory Theatre, and is the flagship – and largest – of the company's three performance venues. The Rep won the 1990 Tony Award for Outstanding Regional Theater, confirming its reputation for producing classic and contemporary plays of high literary standards.

1 Paramount Theatre
MAP K3 ■ 911 Pine St ■ (206) 682-1414 ■ www.stgpresents.org

One of the most treasured theaters in town, the restored Paramount dates from 1928 and exudes the charm of the popular Beaux-Arts style of its period. Today, it presents Broadway shows, jazz and rock concerts, and dance performances.

2 Moore Theatre
Built in 1907, the grand lobby and halls of Seattle's oldest theater is full of mosaics, stained glass, and woodcarvings. In 1974, it was placed on the National Register of Historic Places. It also serves as a base for new rock bands (see p74).

3 ACT Theatre/ Kreielsheimer Place
MAP K4 ■ 700 Union St ■ (206) 292-7676 ■ www.acttheatre.org

Housed in the beautifully refurbished Kreielsheimer Place (formerly the Eagles Auditorium), the long-running A Contemporary Theatre (ACT) showcases contemporary playwrights. Inside, The cultural center contains four performance spaces, administrative offices, rehearsal spaces, and scene and costume shops.

5 McCaw Hall
In 2003, the city's original opera house underwent a massive transformation to become McCaw Hall (see pp14–15). Built for no less than $127 million, this plush 2,900-seat auditorium, with state-of-the-art acoustics and excellent amenities, is home to the Seattle Opera and Pacific Northwest Ballet.

6 KeyArena
The largest indoor venue in Seattle Center is home to the city's professional women's basketball team, the Seattle Storm, and is also a popular venue for major events and concerts (see p15).

Concertgoers fill the KeyArena

7 5th Avenue Theatre

MAP K4 ■ 1308 5th Ave ■ (206) 625-1900 ■ www.5thavenue theatre.org

Opened in 1926 as a vaudeville venue, 5th Avenue has an ornate imperial Chinese design inspired by Beijing's Forbidden City. It is Seattle's home for touring musical theater.

8 Broadway Performance Hall

Victor Steinbrueck, who helped preserve Pike Place Market *(see pp12–13)*, was also instrumental in saving this auditorium *(see p24)* from demolition. Its repertoire includes film festivals, music and dance recitals, and off-the-wall theater.

Dance performance, Sky Church

9 Sky Church

MAP H2 ■ 325 5th Ave N ■ (877) 367-7361 ■ www.mopop.org

This great performance venue at the Museum of Pop Culture *(see pp14–15)* is a 85-ft- (26-m-) high room with 48,000 watts of surround-sound, computer-controlled light systems, and a huge video screen.

10 Benaroya Hall
MAP K4 ■ 200 University St ■ (206) 215-4747 ■ www.seattle symphony.org

This bastion of culture is the city's first venue designed exclusively for music performances. It is also home to the Seattle Symphony. The 2,500-seat Mark Taper auditorium is well known for its acoustics. A 540-seat hall is used for smaller concerts.

TOP 10 BEST CINEMAS

Neptune theater hall

1 Neptune
MAP E2 ■ 1303 NE 45th St ■ (206) 781-5755
Built in 1921, this place has a nautical motif and movie-palace grandeur.

2 Central Cinema
MAP F4 ■ 1411 21st Ave ■ (206) 686-6684
A theatre with food and cocktail service.

3 Northwest Film Forum
This has an independent cinema and studio for incubating new work *(see p80)*.

4 Cinerama
MAP J3 ■ 2100 4th Ave ■ (206) 448-6680
Paul Allen funded this 808-seat cinema.

5 Fremont Outdoor Cinema (Summers)
MAP D2 ■ N 35th & Phinney Ave N ■ (206) 781-4230
A favorite for cult and classic movies.

6 Grand Illusion
MAP E2 ■ 1403 NE 50th St ■ (206) 523-3935
Shows the best of avant-garde cinema.

7 Rendezvous/Jewel Box
This Belltown bar seats only a few die-hard fans of independent film *(see p74)*.

8 Majestic Bay
MAP B1 ■ 2044 NW Market St ■ (206) 781-2229
A vintage theater with modern luxuries.

9 Egyptian Theatre
MAP L3 ■ 805 E Pine St ■ (206) 781-5755
With its kitschy decor, the theater housed SIFF *(see p60)* in the 1980s.

10 Varsity
MAP E2 ■ 4329 University Way NE ■ (206) 781-5755
The Varsity has thrived since 1940.

TOP 10 Outdoor Activities

1 Colman Pool
MAP P2 ■ 8603 Fauntleroy Way SW ■ Open late May–Aug ■ Adm
An alternative to the inhospitable, cold Puget Sound is a dip in Colman Pool. It uses heated and filtered saltwater drawn from the Sound, which it overlooks from its beach location in Lincoln Park (see p46).

Outdoor Colman Pool

2 Kayaking
With its Ship Canal links to Lake Washington and Shilshole, and its proximity to downtown, Lake Union is the most convenient point for kayaking. When there is no wind, the currents are barely an issue, even for novices. More adventurous river-runners find their rapid transit in challenging whitewater courses closer to the mountains.

3 Snowshoe Treks
One of the most popular wintertime sports is snowshoeing, an ancient method of walking on or through the white stuff. The National Park Service and local outfitters offer a series of guided walks. Beginners should start with an experienced professional guide to lead the outing.

4 Climbing Rock Walls
One of the most popular indoor locations for rock climbing is Recreational Equipment Incorporated (REI), which has a huge practice wall in the atrium of its flagship store on Eastlake Avenue. Schurman Rock at Camp Long (see p103) offers outdoor climbing for free for those with gear. Stone Gardens on NW Market Street offers classes and practice walls for both members and walk-ins.

5 Burke-Gilman Trail
The legacy of two of Seattle's earliest railroad men, Judge Thomas Burke and Daniel Gilman, this dis-used railroad is a paved trail (see p93) that stretches 27 miles (43 km) from the western edge of Ballard to the north end of Lake Washington. Cyclists and pedestrians can enjoy the scenic beauty of key sights such as Gas Works Park (see p46) and Magnuson Park at Sand Point.

6 Skiing and Snowboarding
Seattleites wait anxiously for the first large snowfall that carpets ski runs in the Cascades. Crystal Mountain, Alpental, Snoqualmie Pass, and Stevens Pass attract downhill and cross-country skiers, and boarders who have honed their skills on the area's famously chal-lenging snow routes.

Snow-covered Crystal Mountain

Scuba diving in Puget Sound

7 Scuba Diving

For an adventurous sport, opt for scuba diving in Puget Sound to discover undersea creatures such as wolf eels, octopuses, sea stars, and urchins. Divers can embark solo or as part of chartered excursions to take advantage of a coastline that is never victim to damage or dangerous currents from Pacific Ocean storms.

8 Windsurfing

For one of the country's prime windsurfing meccas, head to Hood River, Oregon, in the Columbia River Gorge. Seattle has two prime locations for those who want to be swept away – along the west shores of Lake Washington, between Magnuson Beach and Seward Park; and at Golden Gardens Park, where Shilshole Bay meets Puget Sound.

9 Paddle Boarding

MAP D3 ▪ Urban Surf ▪ 2100 N Northlake Way ▪ www.urbansurf.com

The warmer, protected waters of Lake Union are a perfect place to try this popular watersport. Rental equipment, lessons, and tours are available through Urban Surf.

10 Tolt-MacDonald Park & Campground

MAP Q2 ▪ 31020 NE 40th St, Carnation

Many of Seattle's in-city parks have decent single tracks for casual mountain biking. But intermediate-level cyclists looking for a challenge in a great riverside setting should head 28 miles (45 km) east across Lake Washington to Carnation, in the Snoqualmie River valley.

TOP 10 PLACES TO RENT GEAR

1 REI
MAP K2 ▪ 222 Yale Ave N ▪ (206) 223-1944
This store helped define Seattle as an outdoor recreation mecca.

2 Second Ascent
MAP B2 ▪ 5209 Ballard Ave NW ▪ (206) 545-8810
Offers snowshoes, trekking poles, helmets, plastic boots, ice axes, and crampons rental for the keen climber.

3 Feathered Friends
MAP K2 ▪ 119 Yale Ave N ▪ (206) 292-2210
Has a great selection of climbing gear.

4 Agua Verde Café & Paddle Club
MAP E2 ▪ 1303 NE Boat St ▪ (206) 545-8570
Rent a kayak or dine on Mexican food.

5 Moss Bay Rowing & Kayaking Center
MAP K1 ▪ 1001 Fairview Ave N ▪ (206) 682-2031
Offers a variety of kayaks and rowboats.

6 Gregg's Greenlake Cycles
MAP E1 ▪ 7007 Woodlawn Ave NE ▪ (206) 523-1822
Road bikes are available for hire here.

7 Greenlake Boat Rentals
MAP E1 ▪ 7351 East Green Lake Dr N ▪ (206) 527-0171
Offers stand up paddle boats for rent.

8 Windworks Sailing Center
MAP A1 ▪ 7001 Sea-view Ave NW ▪ (206) 784-9386
Rent bareboats or take sailing lessons.

9 Northwest Outdoor Center
MAP D3 ▪ 2100 Westlake Ave N ▪ (206) 281-9694
Rent kayaks or paddle along the Canal.

10 Center for Wooden Boats
Museum and boat rentals (see p38).

Center for Wooden Boats

TOP 10 Urban Retreats

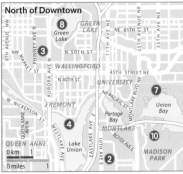

1 Lincoln Park
MAP P3

Located on the road to West Seattle's Fauntleroy Ferry Terminal (see p104), this is a versatile recreational find for those looking for hilly trails, picnics by the water, or even a dip in the outdoor Colman Pool (see p44).

Volunteer Park Conservatory

2 Volunteer Park
MAP E4 ■ 1247 15th Ave E

Between 1904 and 1909, the Olmsted Brothers turned these 45 acres (18 ha) of hilltop into a rustic grass meadow with a fantastic view. The park now houses the Seattle Asian Art Museum (see p38), the Volunteer Park Conservatory, and an observation tower (see p80). It is also a notorious gay pick-up scene at night.

3 Woodland Park Rose Garden

New visitors to the Woodland Park Zoo (see pp30–31) often stumble across this gated area near one of the zoo entrances. Others, nearly a quarter million annually, plan to wake up and smell the roses. About 5,000 individual plants and 280 varieties of rose turn this 2.5-acre (1-ha) corner of Seattle into a technicolor dream.

4 Gas Works Park
MAP D3 ■ 2101 N Northlake Way ■ (206) 684-4075

Set up in 1906 as a gasification plant to light the streets of Seattle, this became the first industrial site in the world to be re-created into a public park. The park has been scrubbed several times over the years. Much of the machinery either remains on exhibit, or sits rusting behind security fences. It has a high kite hill topped with a sundial created by local artists Chuck Greening and Kim Lazare.

5 Schmitz Preserve Park
MAP A5 ■ (206) 684-4075

The scant remains of the temperate rainforest old growth trees hint at what Seattle must have resembled before European settlement. Schmitz is a deep, wide, wooded ravine surrounded by residential streets, but street noises disappear among the magnificent trees and native plants.

6 Kubota Garden

MAP P3 ■ 9817 55th Ave S
■ (206) 725-5060 ■ www.seattle.gov/
parks/find/parks/kubota-garden

Discover 20 acres (8 ha) of traditional Japanese landscaping, with native plants, tucked in a residential neighborhood in South Seattle. With koi ponds, rock and formal bridges, a waterfall, and ever-changing views, this place is a real delight, especially in spring for the blossoms, or in fall for the changing colors of the leaves. It is free to visit and rarely crowded.

7 Center for Urban Horticulture

MAP F2 ■ 3501 NE 41st St

The CUH was established in 1980 by the University of Washington in order to exert more control and achieve sounder management of the arboretum. It includes a herb garden, a library, pleasant meadows, and weekly master-gardener meetings.

8 Green Lake

MAP D1

The well-worn paths in this lake's sylvan setting take visitors around the placid water in a quiet neighborhood north of downtown. Gently rippling with the wind or mirror-smooth, Green Lake's mesmerizing surface allows minds to wander freely. It is usually packed on weekends, especially in the summer months, when people flock to the grassy areas to sunbathe by the lake.

9 Golden Gardens

In Ballard's far northwestern edge along Puget Sound, the wide sandy beaches of Golden Gardens *(see p98)* take on the characteristics of a cherished vacation spot. The Olympic Mountains stand to the west, a marina lies adjacent, and Lake Washington Ship Canal is nearby, so pleasure crafts are always in view. There are wetlands, a wooded area, a stream, and a trail.

The waterfront Golden Gardens

10 Washington Park Arboretum and Japanese Garden

MAP F3 ■ 2300 Arboretum Dr E
■ Japanese Garden: 1075 Lake Washington Blvd E; Adm

The arboretum features 230 acres (93 ha) of carefully cultivated landscapes and rare tree species. The gardens, a living page of Japanese history, were built in 1960 to plans by Japanese designer Juki Iida. These include a traditional sculpture, ponds, and a teahouse *(see p58)*.

Washington Park Japanese Garden

🔟 Off the Beaten Path

1 Jack Block Park
MAP B5 ■ 2130 Harbor Ave SW
■ **Open dawn to dusk**
Not many people know about this park but it offers possibly the best view in Seattle. There is a pier, a small beach, and an overlook towards the city. It is well signposted but most miss it on their way to Alki Beach.

Volunteer Park Water Tower

2 Volunteer Park Water Tower
MAP M1
Those who walk up 107 spiral steps of the Volunteer Park Water Tower will be rewarded with a 360-degree view over the city. Between the tower windows, there are exhibits on Seattle's parks and their landscape architect, Frederick Law Olmstead.

3 SPARK Museum of Electrical Invention
MAP P4 ■ 1312 Bay St, Bellingham ■ (360) 738-3886 ■ www.spark museum.org
Take a drive north to Bellingham to dive into the history of electricity and radio. This delightfully nerdy collection spans objects from the 1600s and the dawn of electricity through to the golden age of radio in the 1950s.

4 West Seattle Farmers' Market
MAP A5 ■ Alaska St & California Ave ■ **Every Sunday** ■ www.seattle farmersmarkets.org/markets/ west-seattle
The city has at least a dozen weekly farmers' markets – this recently expanded one is a good excuse to venture into an underappreciated neighborhood. It is open all year round, but is slightly smaller in winter.

5 Georgetown
MAP P2 ■ Between S Lucile St, W Marginal Way S & Airport Way S
This rapidly changing neighborhood is home to cool diner-style breakfast joints, the Georgetown Trailer Park Mall, the Jules Maes Saloon, Seattle's oldest bar, art galleries and shops, Fran's Chocolates, and seven different breweries.

The modern exterior of the Bainbridge Island Museum of Art

6 Kubota Garden

Worth the detour to Renton, this beautiful Japanese garden was founded by Japanese-born Fujitaro Kubota in 1927, and opened to the public in 1987. His work was interrupted by his internment during World War II; the grounds are still maintained by the Kubota family. This rarely crowded site is especially magical when the cherry blossoms are in flower in springtime (see p47).

7 Seattle Pinball Museum

MAP L6 ■ 508 Maynard Ave S ■ (206) 623-0759 ■ Adm ■ www.seattlepinballmuseum.com

Visitors cannot play the 1939 game on display in the window, but they are free to use almost everything else in the two-floor collection – and play is included with the price of admission. Enjoy all the flashing lights, ringing bells, and rolling counters you can stand.

8 Mimosas Cabaret

MAP L3 ■ (206) 437-2532 ■ 1118 E Pike St ■ Open 1pm Sat–Sun ■ www.mimosascabaret.com

Visit for brunch, drag queens, and accelerated versions of popular Broadway musicals. This Sunday afternoon extravaganza is for anyone who enjoys camp cabaret and stiff drinks, but who also wants to take an afternoon nap. It is raunchy fun for the open minded (and those aged 21 and over). Be sure to bring some small change to tip the performers. Reservations are recommended.

9 Bainbridge Island Museum of Art

MAP N2 ■ 550 Winslow Way E ■ (206) 842-4451 ■ www.biartmuseum.org

Take the ferry downtown and get off at Bainbridge Island to visit this free museum, which showcases the work of local Pacific Northwest artists. It is a very short walk from the museum to the quaint village of Winslow for shopping and refreshments.

10 Lake View Cemetery

This is mostly a destination for those wishing to pay homage to the martial arts master, Bruce Lee, and his son, Brandon. However, it is also a peaceful diversion among the resting places of many Seattle pioneers, including founder Arthur A. Denny and department store magnate John W. Nordstrom (see p80).

The Lees' grave, Lake View Cemetery

🔟 Children's Attractions

1 Seattle Children's Museum

MAP H2 ■ 305 Harrison St ■ (260) 441-1768 ■ Adm ■ www.thechildrens museum.org

In the heart of Seattle Center, this museum contains imaginative galleries and hands-on studio spaces that endlessly stimulate children's imaginations. The Global Village reveals lifestyles of Japan, Ghana, and the Philippines, and the Bijou Theatre invites young performers to dress up and act out scripts.

2 Space Needle

A 41-second glass-elevator ride rockets you up to the observation deck for unforgettable views. Kids will take great delight from the Lunar Orbiter dessert served in the revolving SkyCity restaurant – an over-the-top ice-cream sundae, swathed in clouds of dry ice. It is truly out of this world (see p15).

3 International Fountain

MAP H2 ■ 305 Harrison St ■ (206) 684-7200

During any festival and all through summer, the fountain draws scores of frolicking children. Weather permitting, kids play in the majestic arcs of water projecting out and up from the spherical base, all to music.

International Fountain on a sunny day

Children's Film Festival performers

4 Children's Film Festival Seattle

MAP M3 ■ 1515 12th Ave ■ (206) 829-7863 ■ Adm ■ www.nwfilmforum.org

This ten-day event allows young people and families to enjoy and even judge new feature films. It is held annually, January to February.

5 Seattle Pinball Museum

It will not matter how many balls the kids lose here – they can play as many games as they like for a single admission price. There are more than 50 games, some dating back to the 1960s (see p49).

6 Museum of Flight

Many children like to fly, or fly off the handle. Either way, one way to encourage the former and stifle the latter is to take them to this museum (see p39). It also provides insightful outreach programs for children.

7 Toy Stores

Magic Mouse Toys: MAP K5; 603 1st Ave; (206) 682-8097 ▪ Top Ten Toys: MAP P2; 104 N 85th St; (206) 782-0098

The city's most popular local toy stores have a very loyal following because their toys spur children's imaginations without sparing the fun. Browse the jam-packed aisles at Top Ten Toys and Magic Mouse Toys.

8 Tillicum Village

Blake Island, across the bay from the waterfront, contains a rainforest park and a fabricated Native American village. A four-hour adventure includes the cruise, food, music, and dance, with time to stroll beaches and trails (see p17).

A Ride the Ducks amphibious vehicle

9 Ride the Ducks

MAP H2 ▪ 516 Broad St ▪ (800) 817-1116

These amphibious vehicles from World War II provide an offbeat excursion around the city. Areas include downtown, the Pike Place Market, Pioneer Square, Fremont, and Lake Union's houseboats.

10 Northwest Puppet Center

MAP P2 ▪ 9123 15th Ave NE ▪ (206) 523-2579 ▪ www.nwpuppet.org

Founded by the dedicated Carter Family Marionettes in 1986, this center offers a museum, library, and more than 250 annual performances. The troupe tours and also sponsors educational outreach programs.

TOP 10 HOTELS WITH SWIMMING POOLS

The Fairmont Olympic Hotel

1 Fairmont Olympic Hotel
The indoor pool and spa are just two of many amenities here (see p116).

2 Seattle Marriott Waterfront
This attractive waterfront hotel offers a heated indoor as well as outdoor pool, with views of Puget Sound (see p117).

3 Marriott Courtyard
MAP D4 ▪ 925 Westlake Ave N ▪ (206) 213-0100
Relax in the hot tub while the kids frolic in the indoor pool.

4 Sheraton Seattle
MAP K4 ▪ 1400 6th Avenue ▪ (206) 621-9000
Parents may prefer idle moments in the wine bar, but the hotel also has a heated indoor pool for all ages.

5 The Westin Seattle
The indoor pool here is an all-weather plus, as is the fitness center (see p117).

6 University Inn
Families will appreciate the free breakfast buffet at this inn (see p117).

7 Travelodge Seattle Center
Amenities are few, but there is a children's play area, free breakfast, and an outdoor pool (see p119).

8 Warwick Seattle Hotel
This family-friendly hotel in Belltown has many 24-hour extras and an excellent pool (see p119).

9 The Maxwell Hotel Seattle
Well located, dog-friendly hotel with an indoor pool and cycle hire (see p119).

10 Silver Cloud Inn
MAP M4 ▪ 1100 Broadway ▪ (206) 325-1400
Take advantage of this inn's pool, complimentary breakfasts, and shuttles to downtown.

🔟 Nightlife

1 Dimitriou's Jazz Alley
MAP J3 ▪ 2033 6th Ave
▪ (206) 441-9729

A solid anchor in the Seattle music scene, Dimitriou's Jazz Alley has been bringing the best jazz, swing, and blues musicians to the Pacific Northwest since 1979. Big acts that have performed here include Eartha Kitt, Taj Mahal, Count Basie Orchestra, and Dr. John. There are dinner shows and music-only shows.

Performance at Dimitriou's Jazz Alley

2 El Corazón
MAP L3 ▪ 109 Eastlake Ave E
▪ (206) 262-0482

Formerly known as Graceland, El Corazón proudly flaunts its roots as a crusty, smoky rock club. It is a mecca for many of the area's rock bands.

3 The Triple Door
MAP J4 ▪ 216 Union St
▪ (206) 838-4333

In the space of a former 1920s-era vaudeville theater, upscale audiences soak up the best of live jazz, rock, blues, and cabaret while enjoying Pan-Asian drinks and cuisine.

4 The Showbox
MAP J4 ▪ 1426 1st Ave
▪ (206) 628-0221

An elegant 1900s Art Deco room, with state-of-the-art audio and lighting, The Showbox has been used as a concert hall and comedy club. Artists as dissimilar as Al Jolson, the Mills Brothers, Gypsy Rose Lee, and the Ramones have performed here. Now, the 1,000-seat venue hosts successful rock and hip-hop acts.

5 Nectar Lounge
MAP D2 ▪ 412 N 36th St
▪ (206) 632-2020

A happening Fremont club, Nectar features live music seven nights a week, ranging from indie to hip-hop, reggae to dance, folk, funk, punk, and more. It is host to a good range of national and local acts. There are three bars and an attractive outdoor patio with a fireplace, making this a favorite spot for younger Seattleites. Bar food and a great selection of pizzas are also available.

6 Chop Suey
This club dominates the smoke-filled, hard rock scene on Capitol Hill, but does so with style and flair. Glowing red lights and lanterns shed a little light, while Bruce Lee imagery adds to the kitschy theme. Most of the acts are local or regional rock outfits, although hip-hop rules on Sunday nights *(see p84)*.

Kitsch interior at Chop Suey

Revelers partying at Neumos

7 Neumos
MAP M3 ▪ 925 E Pike St ▪ (206) 709-9467

Once known as Moe's, this is Capitol Hill's trendiest music venue. The club offers indie and classic rock, plus DJ dance nights.

8 Tractor Tavern
MAP B2 ▪ 5213 Ballard Ave NW ▪ (206) 789-3599

A bastion of great music, this place thrives as an alternative to clubs elsewhere in Seattle that are known for hard rock acts. Conversely, the Tractor primarily books bands with repertoire in the vein of country and western, rockabilly, bluegrass, or musicians who seamlessly fuse all those styles into something original.

9 Gallery 1412
MAP E5 ▪ 1412 18th Ave ▪ (206) 322-1533

Gallery 1412 is a collectively owned musical arts venue with an imposing artistic vision. The award-winning curators book acts dedicated to experimental music in a no-frills setting. Patrons listen and learn about contemporary composition, electro-acoustic and electronic music, improvization, and jazz.

10 Sunset Tavern
MAP B1 ▪ 5433 Ballard Ave NW ▪ (206) 784-4880

This tavern is primarily an outlet for start-up bands of the ear-shattering punk rock persuasion. The room's red decor and lighting seems to take inspiration from a Victorian bordello.

TOP 10 LOCAL MICROBREWS

1 Redhook Brewery
MAP E4 ▪ 714 E Pike St ▪ (206) 823-3026
One of the top breweries since 1981.

2 Hale's Ales Brewery
Savor the brews and grub (see p95).

3 Maritime Pacific Brewing Company
MAP C2 ▪ 1111 NW Ballard Way ▪ (206) 782-6181
Order a pint of Nightwatch here.

4 Elliott Bay Brewing Company
MAP A6 ▪ 4720 California Ave SW ▪ (206) 932-8695
This is West Seattle's bastion of microbrews and pub fare.

5 McMenamins Six Arms
MAP E4 ▪ 300 E Pike St ▪ (206) 223-1648
Six Arms is a popular branch of the McMenamins microbrew chain.

6 Elysian Brewing Company
The Hill's best pub makes its own legendary brews (see p84).

7 Pyramid Alehouse, Brewery & Restaurant
MAP D6 ▪ 1201 1st Ave S ▪ (206) 682-3377
Great beers and faux-Egyptian labels.

8 Big Time Brewery & Alehouse
MAP E2 ▪ 4133 University Way NE ▪ (206) 545-4509
Sample handcrafted ales here.

9 Mac & Jack's
MAP P2 ▪ 17825 NE 65th St, Redmond ▪ (425) 558-9697
Try their great African Amber.

10 Pike Brewing Company
MAP J4 ▪ 1415 1st Ave ▪ (206) 622-6044
Best for microbrews, pub food, or for purchasing brewing supplies.

Beer from Pike Brewing Company

🔟 Restaurants

Wonderful high ceilings at Lark

1 Lark

Located In a converted 1917 warehouse with 25-ft- (7.6-m-) high ceilings, chef John Sundstrom's Lark is one of the Pacific Northwest's most lauded restaurants, known for working with local farmers to provide seasonal dishes. The menu features delicious and fresh small plates of locally produced cheese, vegetables, charcuterie, and fish *(see p85)*.

2 Metropolitan Grill

MAP K5 ▪ 820 2nd Ave ▪ (206) 624-3287 ▪ $$$

One of Seattle's most loved and traditional steakhouses draws in a faithful group of politicians and corporate attorneys every day. Portions are typically huge – salads, appetizers, baked potatoes, everything features – so bring lots of friends for sharing.

Wagyu beef dish, Metropolitan Grill

3 Ray's Boathouse & Café

This Ballard waterfront restaurant has two dining rooms. The café caters to happy-hour revelers, families, and informal diners, while the boathouse offers reservation-only seating. Both menus include the freshest Dungeness crab, oysters, and wild Alaskan salmon *(see p101)*.

4 Café Juanita

MAP P2 ▪ 9702 NE 120th Place, Kirkland ▪ (425) 823-1505 ▪ $$$

This award-winning restaurant in Kirkland is renowned for its passion for Northern Italian food and wine. The lengthy menu reflects the kitchen's commitment to organic, sustainable ingredients. Exceptional service and a calm, classy dining room complete the experience.

5 Canlis

MAP D3 ▪ 2576 Aurora Ave N ▪ (206) 283-3313 ▪ $$$

Treat your eyes and palate to a special dinner at Canlis. Specialties include Alaska halibut, Dungeness crab, Wagyu-style tenderloin, and a comprehensive and expensive wine selection. For an even more memorable occasion, reserve the private cache room for two, and order in advance to ensure a serving of the luscious chocolate lava cake.

6 Dahlia Lounge

Owner-chef Tom Douglas was one of the Seattle area's first fusion chefs, blending flavors into cohesive and tasty concoctions. Traditional dinner items such as crab cakes are favorites *(see p77)*. Next door is the sweet tooth's haven, Dahlia Bakery.

7 The Herbfarm

MAP P2 ▪ 14590 NE 145th St, Woodinville ▪ (425) 485-5300 ▪ $$$

Dining at this Eastside restaurant requires time, money, and an appreciation of the culinary arts.

For a key to restaurant price ranges see p77

Chef Chris Weber's kitchen often uses ingredients from the restaurant's gardens and farm. Creative menus include a nine-course dinner of Northwest foods, served with five or six matched wines (non-alcoholic options are also available). Be sure to reserve well in advance.

8 The Brooklyn Seafood, Steak & Oyster House

MAP K4 ▪ 1212 2nd Ave ▪ (206) 395-9227 ▪ $$

The not-to-be-missed dish here is the platter of fresh local oysters. Classic cocktails are served at great prices during happy hour, and the consistently excellent service completes the experience at this centrally located, buzzing spot.

9 Sitka & Spruce

MAP L3 ▪ 1531 Melrose Ave ▪ (206) 324-0662 ▪ $$

There is an open kitchen producing seasonally selected dishes with an Italian twist in an industrial-style interior at this eatery. Locally sourced ingredients are prominent on the menu. Found in Capitol Hill's Melrose Market, a hip collective of stores and restaurants, it is very popular so be sure to make a reservation.

10 The Walrus and the Carpenter

Try the steak tartare and the freshly caught oysters, washed down with great cocktails at this crowded, trendy seafood restaurant. Expect to have to line up on weekends; there are no reservations *(see p101)*.

The Walrus and the Carpenter

TOP 10 CAFÉS

Herkimer Coffee sign

1 Herkimer Coffee
MAP P2 ▪ 7320 Greenwood N ▪ (206) 784-0202
A tastefully designed coffee shop.

2 Bauhaus Strong Coffee
MAP B1 ▪ 2001 NW Market St ▪ (206) 453-3068
Home-roasted coffee and pastries.

3 Caffé Ladro
MAP E4 ▪ 435 15th Ave E ▪ (206) 267-0551
A local chain with excellent espressos.

4 Zeitgeist
MAP K6 ▪ 171 S Jackson ▪ (206) 583-0497
This place makes exceptional espresso and also sponsors art shows.

5 Little Oddfellows
Café in the Elliott Bay Book Co. *(see p83).*

6 Fremont Coffee Company
MAP D2 ▪ 459 N 36th ▪ (206) 632-3633
Superb coffee and tasty wraps.

7 Lighthouse Roasters
MAP D2 ▪ 400 N 43rd ▪ (206) 634-3140
Rich drinks are made from freshly roasted coffee beans.

8 Café Allegro
MAP E2 ▪ 4214 University Way NE ▪ (206) 633-3030
Keeps students, professors, and locals stoked on perfectly brewed coffee.

9 Café Besalu
MAP B1 ▪ 5909 24th Ave NW ▪ (206) 789-1463
This European-style café lures foodies with its gourmet pastries.

10 Cederberg Tea House
The perfect place to enjoy afternoon tea and snacks *(see p84).*

📼 Stores and Shopping Centers

① 5th Avenue Boutiques

MAP K4

A collection of boutiques between Union and Spring Streets caters for customers for whom price is no object. Fox's Gem Shop, Brooks Brothers, and St. John Boutique are the best stops for fine gems, jewelry, and high fashion galore.

② Macy's

MAP J4 ▪ 1601 3rd Ave
▪ (206) 506-6000

For less extravagant spenders, there is what used to be the locally owned Bon Marché. The new name reflects investment and ownership by the famous Chicago department store chain, but locals still refer to this large store simply as the Bon. Find everything from linen to lingerie and luggage, all at reasonable prices.

③ Westlake Center

MAP K4 ▪ 400 Pine St
▪ (206) 467-1600

This shopping center has a four-tiered glass-enclosed atrium stacked with small locally based shops, chain stores, and a large food court. Made in Washington, Fireworks, Mix, Jessica McClintock, Lush, and Nature's are well worth visiting. Outside, Westlake Plaza attracts workers on break, and also features seasonal concerts and events.

Westlake Center

The Apple Store at University Village

④ University Village

MAP F2 ▪ 4500 25th Ave NE
▪ (206) 523-0622

This urban shopping center just east of the UW has lovely landscaped walkways, fountains, restaurants, and stores that no longer attract just the resident graduate student population. Stores include an Apple Store, Nike Running, Warby Parker, RH Gallery, Madewell, and Din Tai Fung.

⑤ Nordstrom

MAP K4 ▪ 500 Pine St
▪ (206) 628-2111

John W. Nordstrom's *(see p37)* shoe store, opened with his Alaskan gold rush earnings in 1901, is now synonymous with impeccable service and quality merchandise. Hunting for fine apparel, exquisite handbags, elegant shoes, or other accessories can be exhausting, so step into the in-store spa and salon to recover.

⑥ North of the Market to Belltown

MAP J4

A stroll along First and Second avenues in the Belltown area leads to this ultrahip shopping destination. There are boutique shoe stores, upscale bathroom fixtures and furnishing stores, art galleries, and many other intriguing stores for curious shoppers. And, when a rest is needed, there is no shortage of restaurants, coffee shops, or bars.

7 Wallingford Center
MAP D2 ■ 1815 N 45th St
■ (206) 517-7773

For a real taste of Seattle's charming Wallingford neighborhood, discover a variety of local commerce along 45th Street, such as restaurants and shops, as well as the Wallingford Center, an early-19th-century elementary school. Quite a few of these shops are for (or about) children, including L'il Klippers hair salon.

8 Melrose Market
MAP L2 ■ 1501–1535 Melrose Ave

Housed in a series of former automotive repair buildings, this chic upscale indoor-outdoor market includes several trendy restaurants, a meat market, home decor and gift shops, as well as a clothing boutique and spirits shop.

9 Pacific Place
MAP K3 ■ 600 Pine St
■ (206) 405-2655

Part of a $500-million development plan, Pacific Place is the crown jewel of Seattle's retail shopping centers. Stores include Tiffany & Co., Coach, Ann Taylor, Guess, Lulumon, Aveda, L'Occitane, and Williams-Sonoma. The top level has an 11-screen AMC Theatre complex and several fine gourmet

restaurants. To top it off, there is also a skybridge connection to the Nordstrom flagship store.

10 Westfield Southcenter
MAP P3 ■ 2800 Southcenter Mall ■ (206) 246-0423

With more than 200 shops and services, this is the largest shopping center in the Pacific Northwest. Key stores include JCPenney, Nordstrom, Sears, J.Crew, Abercrombie & Fitch, Pandora, Bebe, Macy's, and Sephora. There are also plenty of restaurants, a food court facing Mount Rainier, a 16-screen AMC movie theater, and a rainforest-themed play area for kids. The mall is located in the suburban city of Tukwila, close to the airport.

The large, glass-roof atrium of Pacific Place, one of Seattle's top malls

TOP10 Seattle for Free

Washington Park Arboretum

1 Washington Park Arboretum and Japanese Garden

The plants here range from sprawling big leaf maples to the water lilies in Duck Bay, which also a good place for turtle spotting. There is an entry fee for the Japanese Garden but the rest of the grounds are free to explore. It is especially nice in fall when the leaves change (see p47).

2 Center for Wooden Boats Sunday Public Sailing

Sprit boats, steamboats, electric boats, schooners, ketches, yawls, and yachts: the fleet varies, but they sail every Sunday. It is first come first served, so show up early (see p38).

3 Discovery Park

Trails zigzag across the bluffs of the park and down to the rocky beach on Puget Sound, offering gorgeous views across the water to the Olympic Mountains (see pp32–3).

4 Northwest Folklife Festival

Enjoy three days of international food, music, storytelling, and theater at this free festival. The aim is to celebrate the communities that make up the Pacific Northwest and the arts they create. It is crowded, but always fun (see p60).

5 Ballard Fish Ladder
MAP C2 ▪ 3015 NW 54th St
▪ (206) 780-2500

Forward thinking conservationist Hiram M. Chittenden understood that the building of a passageway to help ships reach the inland shipyards would disrupt the salmon migration, so he built this underwater staircase to help them. The peak season for salmon viewing in the underwater viewing gallery is July to November.

6 First Thursday Art Walk
MAP K5 ▪ Pioneer Square
▪ www.pioneersquare.org/experiences/first-thursday-art-walk

Explore Seattle's great contemporary art scene on the first Thursday of every month, when all the Pioneer Square galleries open their doors to introduce new exhibitions and artists. Pick up a gallery guide at any of the Pioneer Square galleries and enjoy the people-watching.

7 Frye Art Museum

This small, privately funded museum (see p38) on First Hill displays frequently changing exhibitions of contemporary art, and a salon-style permanent collection. Try not to be fooled by the traditional nature of the permanent collection – the temporary exhibits can be avant-garde. There is also a good café on site for snacks and refreshments.

Frye Art Museum collection

⑧ Gates Foundation Discovery Center

MAP H2 ■ 440 Fifth Avenue North ■ (206) 709-3100 ■ www.gates foundation.org/Visitor-Center

Hands-on exhibits engage visitors in solving real-world problems around poverty, education, and health. The center explores the work of Bill and Melinda Gates, and invites visitors to think of solutions to the biggest issues facing the world today.

⑨ Central Library

Architect Rem Koolhaas designed the angular, glass-and-steel central library *(see p72)*, which is home to site-specific public art, including an acid-green wall backed with video displays, and a letter-press-inspired floor. No library card is required, and there are lots of free events, too.

Modern design of the Central Library

⑩ Olympic Sculpture Park

This open-air sculpture garden has monumental works of art *(see p17)*, including an enormous Richard Serra installation that kids seem to love, and a whimsical typewriter eraser by Claes Oldenburg. It is a diverting outdoor space, especially on summer evenings.

TOP 10 BUDGET TIPS

Seattle's light rail

1 Skip the Car
Get an ORCA pass and use public transit. Light rail runs from the airport into downtown Seattle.

2 Check Out a Food Court
Seattle Center, Uwajimaya Market, and Crossroads Mall all have good food that costs less than it does in a formal restaurant.

3 Go on Thursday
Many of Seattle's museums are free (excluding special exhibitions) on the first Thursday of every month.

4 Get a CityPASS
This pass allows entry to Seattle's most popular attractions, saving money.

5 Find a Happy Hour
On weeknights, bars and restaurants have discounted menus between about 4pm and 6pm.

6 Picnic
Check out Pike Place and farmers' markets across the city, then stock up on local goodies and head for a park.

7 Stay in a Neighborhood
Centrally located hotels are more convenient, but money can be saved by choosing a place farther out.

8 Check The Stranger
Seattle's independent arts and culture newspaper lists the low- and no-cover bars. It also features a number of great free events around town every week.

9 Eat Globally
International cuisine offerings – Thai, Ethiopian, Vietnamese, Indian etc. – tend to cost less than locally sourced celebrity chef plates.

10 Be a Bookworm
World-class writers read and tell stories in Seattle bookstores for free. Often there is a top notch café on site.

TOP10 Festivals and Parades

1 Seattle Improvised Music Festival (SIMF)
Feb ■ www.waywardmusic.org

The largest and longest-running music festival of its kind anywhere, SIMF is dedicated to the esoteric art of spontaneous composition. Local performers join eclectic international musicians to improvise sets that defy category, but always impress.

The stage at Bumbershoot

2 Bumbershoot
Labor Day weekend ■ www. bumbershoot.com

Performers from all over the world converge for this festival (see p14) for three days packed with concerts, theater productions, independent film screenings, and literary events.

3 Seattle Maritime Festival
May ■ www.seattlemaritime101.com

Enthusiasts of tugboats and ships flock to this festival. It makes for a free, fun, and family-friendly way to learn how the working waterfront has become a major factor in the city's economy and culture. The fair centers around the Bell Street Pier, which is a short walk north from the Seattle Aquarium (see p16) on Pier 59. An exciting and fun highlight is the tugboat race on Elliott Bay.

4 University District Street Fair
May ■ www.udistrictstreetfair.org

Dating from 1970, Seattle's first street fair stretches over ten blocks of "The Ave" and its sidestreets.

Crafts booths, food vendors, and local rock music performances attract families from all over town and beyond.

5 Northwest Folklife Festival
Memorial Day weekend ■ www. nwfolklife.org

A free celebration of the Pacific NW's ethnic music, dance, and arts and crafts, Folklife is a magnet for old (and new) hippies in the region (see p58).

6 Seattle International Film Festival (SIFF)
May–Jun ■ www.siff.net

One of the most respected film festivals in the US, SIFF screens more than 400 new works from at least 60 countries. Even midnight showings of cult films sell out, and notable directors attend screenings.

7 Fremont Fair Solstice Parade
Late Jun ■ www.fremontartscouncil. org

All floats at this parade must be entirely human-powered, stimulating the imaginations of Fremont's arts community. Crews propel samba bands, dancers, and rock quartets using battery-operated amplifiers.

The Fremont Fair Solstice parade

Seattle Pride March performer

 Seattle Pride March
Late Jun ■ www.seattlepride.org

The Seattle Pride March runs from Westlake Park to Seattle Center. Sponsored by the LGBTQ community, it attracts huge crowds from every orientation. Expect outrageous floats, dancing, and the very popular "Dykes on Bikes," a motorcycle outfit whose members freely show what they have beneath the leather.

 Seafair
Late Jul ■ www.seafair.com

A parade along 4th Avenue is a highlight of Seafair, a celebration of maritime and aviation history. Events include displays from Navy's Blue Angels F/A-18 fighter pilots, an All Nations Pow-Wow at Daybreak Cultural Center, hydroplane races on Lake Washington, and battleships open to the public on the waterfront.

 Earshot Jazz Festival
Oct–Nov ■ www.earshot.org

The shoestring staff at the nonprofit Earshot Jazz Festival present a well-respected event. The festivals have consistently showcased successful and emerging jazz artists, enriching the Seattle community at large.

TOP 10 FESTIVALS AND CULTURAL EVENTS

1 Têt Festival
A colorful beginning in late January marks the Vietnamese Lunar New Year.

2 Irish Week Festival
wo days of authentic Irish culture around St. Patrick's Day in mid-March.

3 Seattle Cherry Blossom and Japanese Cultural Festival
Dance, music, martial arts, and tea ceremonies are the highlights of this mid-April fair.

4 Festival Sundiata
Seattle's June celebration of the West African Mansa of the Mali Empire, represents African and African-American cultural traditions.

5 Pagdiriwang Philippine Festival
Philippine independence is marked in mid-June with a festival of dance, film, drama, and culinary arts.

6 BrasilFest
Expect infectious rhythms, dance, and spicy flavors when celebrating this Brazilian Folklore Day in late August.

7 TibetFest
This late August festival preserves Tibet's rituals and traditions while incorporating cultural elements of its neighboring countries.

8 Festa Italiana
This late September festival is all about Italian-style fun and food.

9 Día de Muertos
Pay tribute to your ancestors Latin American style, with altars, artwork, food, and music in early November.

10 Hmong New Year
November marks the end of harvest, a time for relaxing and preparing special foods for the Hmong community.

Dragon costume at Têt Festival

🔟 The Eastside

Seattle's two floating bridges

1 Floating Bridges
MAP P2

Lake Washington's famous floating bridges, the Interstate 90 and the State Route 520 toll bridge, connect Seattle with the suburb of Bellevue and the Eastside. Both highways resemble ordinary bridges except for their middle portions, which rest on the water's surface above air-filled pontoons that support tons of traffic and concrete. Occasional windstorms push waves of water onto the road, creating back ups for commuters.

2 Kirkland
MAP P2

Once a small rural town across Lake Washington, Kirkland has grown into a sprawling suburb with the resident Microsoft executives and managers giving it a reputation for expensive real estate. It is also known for its charming waterfront that offers great shopping and dining options along with fantastic beaches that provide ample views of Seattle and the Olympic Mountains beyond.

3 Microsoft Visitor Center
MAP P2 ▪ 15010 NE 36th St, Redmond ▪ (425) 703-6214

Learn more about the history, products, and vision of the software giant at this high-tech visitor center located on the Redmond campus.

Big screens, interactive exhibits, and a 30-year timeline bring the culture of Microsoft to life. Visitors can check out the latest developments in gaming, mobile devices, and more.

4 Luther Burbank Park
MAP P2 ▪ 2040 84th Ave SE, Mercer Island

Mercer Island is a small affluent community off Interstate 90 near Lake Washington's eastern shore. The lovely waterfront park, on the northeastern tip of the island, offers boaters and visitors many notable attractions such as tennis courts, a playground, and trails that lead to a swimming area and fishing dock. On Sunday afternoons in the summer, the park hosts theater productions and free concerts in its amphitheater.

5 The Gates' Estate
MAP P2 ▪ 1835 73rd Ave NE, Medina

So many people wonder how and where one of the world's richest men lives. Microsoft's founder, Bill Gates, built his estate on Lake Washington's eastern shore, installing the latest technological advancements in modern living – high-end security systems, customized touch and voice controls, and luxurious entertainment facilities. The estate is not open to the public, but it is visible from the water, and touring boats occasionally cruise within sight from a considerable distance.

View of Seattle from Old Bellevue

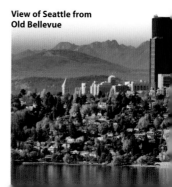

⑥ Eastside Wineries

Chateau Ste. Michelle: MAP P2; 14111 NE 145th St, Woodinville

Michelle, Washington state's oldest winery. Their 87-acre (35-ha) wooded estate in Woodinville, 15 miles (24 km) north of Seattle, hosts tours and well-attended summer concerts. It is one of several outfits taking advantage of a climate that favors excellent grape varieties. Other producers of good-quality wine include Columbia Crest, DeLille Cellars, the Betz Family Winery, and Finn Hill Winery.

⑦ Mercer Slough Nature Park

MAP P2 ▪ 2102 Bellevue Way SE, Bellevue

This 320-acre (129-ha) park on the grounds of the largest remaining wetland on Lake Washington has a 7-mile (11-km) network of trails and esplanades. Bird-watchers flock to the Slough to view 100 species; other wildlife includes coyote, beaver, and muskrat. Activities comprise canoeing and kayaking, guided nature walks and pick-your-own blueberries during summer.

⑧ Old Bellevue

MAP P2

Bellevue is a classic suburb, as well as one of the state's largest cities. But there is an area that harks back to its former life as a small town. Head to Old Bellevue and its charming, restored Main Street for the antidote to freeway interchanges and big box stores, especially if you like buying antiques.

⑨ Marymoor Park

MAP P2 ▪ 6046 W Lake Sammamish Pkwy NE, Redmond

The county's most popular park, located in Redmond, maintains soccer and baseball fields, a velodrome, and a dog-training field, where dogs are free to roam off the leash. Park trails connect with the Sammamish River Trail, a bike route that leads to popular wineries in Woodinville.

⑩ The Bellevue Collection

MAP P2 ▪ 575 Bellevue Sq ▪ (425) 646-3660 ▪ www.bellevue collection.com

These three indoor shopping malls are connected by glass bridges and contain dozens of restaurants and 250 shops, many of them upscale boutiques. There is a 65-ft (20-m) indoor waterfall and a kids play area. Take express bus (550) from downtown Seattle to get here.

TOP 10 Day Trips: Islands and Historic Towns

1 Vashon Island
MAP N3

This island's gentle, two-lane roads make it a favorite for both cyclists and motorcyclists looking for a countryside getaway. Board the Fauntleroy Ferry (see p104) to visit the island's estates, arts and crafts galleries, berry and alpaca farms, and a subculture of 1960s-style progressives.

Point Robinson Light, Vashon Island

2 Victoria, BC
MAP N4

Catch a ferry or seaplane to British Columbia's capital, Victoria. Founded as a Hudson's Bay Company fur-trading post in 1843, it has become a favorite destination for Anglophiles who line up at the grand Fairmont Empress Hotel for traditional tea and cakes. Other attractions include the Inner Harbor, the Royal British Columbia Museum, and Butchart Gardens – an amazing collection of flora planted in a sprawling former quarry.

3 Whidbey Island
MAP P1

As the longest island in the western United States, Whidbey Island's ample waterfront real estate makes it vacation-home central. The island's six state parks, historic forts, and seaside villages attract weekend crowds. It is also the perfect location for the area's largest US Navy air base. Its sign reads, "Pardon our noise, it's the sound of freedom".

4 Port Townsend
MAP N1

This idyllic seaport, on the northeast tip of the Olympic Peninsula, attracts artists and musicians. Known for its Victorian architecture, the town includes Jefferson County Historical Society, Ann Starrett Mansion, Fire Bell Tower, and Fort Worden State Park among its key sights. There is a bustling waterfront with stores, restaurants, cafés, and a ferry terminal.

5 Olympia
MAP P6

Washington's state capital has a rich past, historic buildings, and a thriving youth culture. Highlights include the State Capitol Campus, with grounds designed by the Olmsted Brothers in 1928; Evergreen State College; a farmers' market; the surrounding, mostly rural, Thurston County; and a number of art venues and theaters.

Washington State Capitol, Olympia

Tulip field in the Skagit Valley

6 La Conner and the Skagit Valley

MAP P4 ■ (888) 642-9284 ■ www.lovelaconner.com

Located around 70 miles (110 km) north of Seattle, the Skagit Valley is the second-largest tulip-producing region in the world after the Netherlands. La Conner, a small community surrounded by flower fields some 20 miles (30 km) west of the Skagit Valley, has several art galleries and cafés with lovely water views. One of the best ways to enjoy this corner of Washington is to rent a bicycle and pedal the area during peak flower season, typically in April. An annual tulip festival celebrates the blooms throughout the month.

7 Tacoma

MAP P3

Founded as a sawmill town in 1852, Tacoma is known for its historic buildings, which include the 1893 Italianate tower of Old City Hall. The magnificent, colorful Chihuly Bridge of Glass links the Museum of Glass to downtown Tacoma and the imaginative Washington State History Museum. Explore the small but impressive Tacoma Art Museum, and Point Defiance Zoo and Aquarium, highlighting a Pacific Rim theme.

8 Bainbridge Island

MAP N2

The scenic ferry ride to Winslow on Bainbridge Island (from downtown Seattle's Pier 52) should be mandatory for tourists who are after an inspiring view of the Seattle skyline. The short stroll from the terminal to Winslow's quaint waterfront stores and cafés has its own rewards.

9 Roslyn

MAP Q6

The model for Cicely, Alaska, in the Emmy-award-winning 1990s television show *Northern Exposure*, Roslyn has its own history unrelated to the quirky profiles offered in Hollywood's depiction. In this mining boomtown, late 19th-century coal companies imported workers of various nationalities, as is evident from the tombs in the cemetery, grouped into 26 "segregated" areas. Roslyn is on the National Register of Historic Places.

10 Leavenworth

MAP Q5

In an effort to revive the struggling logging town, civic leaders remodeled buildings in 1960s Bavarian-style, turning it into a top tourist attraction. Today, the town bustles with festivals, art shows, and summer theater productions. Another popular attraction is the Leavenworth Nutcracker Museum and its 6,000 nutcrackers.

🔟 Day Trips: Mountain Getaways

View over Snoqualmie Falls

1 Snoqualmie Falls
MAP Q2

The Native American tribes regarded Snoqualmie Falls as a sacred place. The 268-ft- (82-m-) high waterfall, beautifully divided by a convenient rock outcropping, marks the end of the Cascade Plateau, where the Snoqualmie River begins its final descent to the sea, 40 miles (65 km) north at Everett. An observation deck and a steep path to the river allow for close-up breathtaking views.

2 Mount Rainier
MAP P6

This silent, snowcapped sentinel, the centerpiece of Mount Rainier National Park, is an awe-inspiring active volcano rising 14,410 ft (4,392 m) above sea level. The grande dame of the Cascades commands great respect for its potentially devastating force; it has more glacial ice – and populated surrounds – than St Helens.

3 Denny Creek
MAP Q5

Hiking near Snoqualmie Pass along I-90 is a mecca for families with kids. The creek pours over a series of rocks and creates swimming pools.

4 Twin Falls
MAP Q5

Hikers in search of deep woods head to Olallie State Park, where a 3-mile (5-km) trail to Twin Falls awaits. The park features giant ferns and salmonberry, and some of the Cascades' few old-growth trees: one Douglas fir has a circumference of 14 ft (4 m).

5 Issaquah Alps
MAP Q3

These foothills west of the Cascades are remnants of mountains that pre-date the more-visited peaks to the east. Cougar, Squak, Tiger, and Rattlesnake Mountains are four main park areas that attract those seeking woodland walks without the altitude.

6 Mount Si
MAP Q3

Seattle's closest Cascade Mountain, Mount Si sits just past Issaquah. The hike is steep but not too difficult, and the views of the Snoqualmie Valley watershed and I-90 are rewarding.

7 Hurricane Ridge
MAP N5

Drive to this 5,230-ft (1,594-m) mountaintop at one of Olympic

The majestic Mount Rainier

National Park's most-visited sites. The paved routes bring visitors to one of the best 360-degree Alpine overlooks. In winter, when the snowpack is deep, the roads remain open for skiers and snowshoers.

⑧ Staircase Rapids
MAP N5

The ferry crossing and subsequent scenic drive along the Hood Canal enhance the journey to these rapids. The popular route inches near the fast-flowing Skokomish River as it pours down the eastern slopes of the Olympic Range on its way to Lake Cushman. Look out for birds, inlcuding kingfishers and harlequin ducks, and giant salamanders on the 2-mile (3-km) loop.

Kingfisher, Staircase Rapids

⑨ Tonga Ridge
MAP Q5

The 6-mile (10-km) trail in the Alpine Lakes Wilderness offers a pleasant walk through forests and wild-berry picking (when in season). Meadows bloom in late spring, and mountain scenery abounds.

⑩ Big Four Ice Caves
MAP P5

Global warming has taken a toll on ice caves, but the attraction at the base of 6,153-ft (1,875-m) Big Four Mountain in the North Cascades is still vital. Hike the 1-mile (1.6-km) trail off the Mountain Loop Highway to the Ice Caves, the unusual result of Alpine avalanches and climate conditions impacting the ice field.

TOP 10 FEATURES OF MOUNT RAINIER

Hikers walking through Paradise

1 Paradise
This area leads to wildflower-filled meadows, and trails starting at 5,400-ft (1,646-m) to moraines and majestic views of the Nisqually Glacier.

2 Sunrise
Recommended as the starting point for solitary hikes, this is reachable by car.

3 Summit Climb
A round trip to the crater and back requires training, professional gear, and takes a few days. Those who are not seasoned climbers should rent a guide or go with a group.

4 Family Day Hikes
Dozens of trails for family day trips and picnics are available; try one out near the Carbon River entrance.

5 Wonderland Trail
This 93-mile (149-km) trail through several mini-ecosystems around the mountain is ideal for serious backpackers with weeks to spare.

6 Cloud Lid
Rainier's cloud cover often resembles a flying saucer hovering above the peak.

7 Glacial Melting
Climate changes have decreased the area of Rainier's permanent snowcap and has facilitated glacial retreats.

8 Jökulhlaups and Lahars
These glacial floods and debris flows, typical of Rainier, can move at speeds of up to 60 mph (95.5 kmph).

9 Sleeping Giant
Experts agree that it is a question of when, and not if, Mount Rainier's active volcano will blow again.

10 Effects of Pollution
Smog from traffic increasingly obscures the mountain.

Seattle
Area by Area

Tlingit totem pole in
Pioneer Square Park

TOP 10 Downtown

What strikes many visitors to downtown Seattle is how easy it is to see the sights, since many of the key attractions lie within easy walking distance of one another. Bookended by Belltown to the north and Pioneer Square to the south, the downtown area can be explored on foot or with the help of the city's excellent bus network. The waterfront boasts many attractions and seafood restaurants on its piers, as well as superb views. Although it is primarily a business district full of skyscrapers, downtown offers a wide range of options for visitors – including gourmet restaurants, attractive shopping centers, upscale boutiques, and world-class galleries and art museums. Downtown is the perfect base from which to explore the city.

Seattle's impressive Central Library

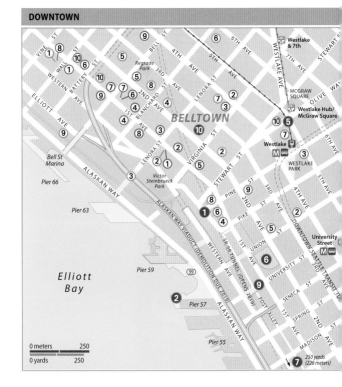

DOWNTOWN

① Pike Place Market

Anyone descending on Pike Place Market – to stroll by innumerable stalls of seafood, fresh produce, crafts, and flower bouquets – can feel the rapid pulse of a scene that is all about the hustle. The market is famous for its salmon-throwing fishmongers and street musicians who entertain tourists daily (see pp12–13).

② Seattle Great Wheel

At the end of Pier 57, on the Seattle waterfront, the Ferris wheel (see p17) sits 175 ft (53 m) above the pier and extends nearly 40 ft (12 m) over Elliott Bay. The 360-degree views are spectacular from all of the 42 climate-controlled, fully enclosed gondolas and each one holds eight people. A ride includes three rotations, each lasting between

Seattle Great Wheel on Pier 57

12–20 minutes, and for an extra cost, a VIP gondola is available, with leather seating and a glass bottom. Night rides are especially notable for the view of Seattle's lights.

③ Washington State Convention Center/ Freeway Park

MAP K4 ■ 705 Pike Street ■ (206) 694-5000 ■ www.wscc.com

Straddling the 10-lane Interstate 5 in a miraculous feat of engineering, the Washington State Convention Center is located within easy walking distance of the city's best stores, hotels, and restaurants. Marvel at the 90-ft- (27-m-) wide glass canopy bridge that frames views to Elliott Bay and to the historic Pike-Pine neighborhood. Adjoining is Freeway Park, where blossoms delight visitors in spring, and waterfalls mask the sounds of traffic flowing on all sides.

Washington State Convention Center

DENNY HILL REGRADE

Named after one of the city's founders, Arthur A. Denny, Denny Hill would have certainly become one of Seattle's most upscale neighborhoods, with magnificent city, mountain, and water views. However, in 1905, the city began removing and regrading the land to allow access to the rest of the city's neighborhoods. Today, the 50-square-block area includes most of what is now called Belltown, and is occupied largely by condos, restaurants, and social agencies.

4 Central Library

MAP K5 ■ 1000 4th Ave ■ Open 10am–8pm Mon–Sat (to 6pm Sat), noon–6pm Sun ■ www.spl.org

Nearly 8,000 patrons per day benefit from more than 1.45 million books and reference materials, and more than 400 public computers at the city's main library. The art collection alone is valued at $1 million (see p40).

5 Seattle Center Monorail

For an adventurous and fun way to travel the 1 mile (1.6 km) between downtown's Westlake Center and the Seattle Center, hop aboard what engineers perceived as the future of mass transit. The first commercial monorail in the US was built as an attraction for the 1962 World's Fair, it still uses the original cars, and makes the short journey every ten minutes (see p41).

6 Seattle Art Museum

MAP J4 ■ 1300 First Ave ■ (206) 654-3100 ■ Open 10am–5pm Wed–Sun (to 9pm Thu) ■ Adm (free 1st Thu of month) ■ www.seattle artmuseum.org

Designed by Venturi Scott Brown and Associates, the imposing sandstone and limestone edifice is now connected seamlessly to the spacious and light-filled 2007 expansion, designed by Brad Cloepfil of Allied Works Architecture. Seattle Art Museum now accommodates major touring exhibitions, as well as an impressive permanent collection of over 23,000 works of ancient to modern art (see p38). The museum's Olympic Sculpture Park (see p17), located at the north end of downtown, showcases unique sculptures in a stunning waterfront setting.

7 Pioneer Square

Find art galleries, intricate Victorian architecture, bookstores, and cafés in a constantly changing National Historic District (see pp18–19). Pioneer Square's 20-block neighborhood became Seattle's commercial center during the boom years of logging, fishing, railroads, and Klondike Gold Rush economies. A 90-minute underground tour offers a lively look at the 19th-century storefronts. A key sight is the Smith Tower, and art lovers will enjoy an art walk that takes place on the first Thursday of each month (see p58).

Seattle Center Monorail train

8 Columbia Center
MAP K5 ■ 701 5th Ave
■ **Observation deck: (206) 386-5564; open 9am–10pm daily; adm**

The sleek, three-tiered skyscraper that dominates Seattle's skyline might have been even taller, but for an order from the Federal Aviation Administration to reduce the final height (see p40).

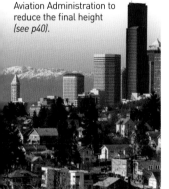

Columbia Center tower

9 Harbor Steps
MAP J5

If you happen to be near the Seattle Art Museum on 1st Avenue and need to get down to the waterfront, try the Harbor Steps. A street's abrupt end has been turned into a wide-open stairway, landscaped with water sculpture and planters. The steps are an ideal urban meeting place, located below a luxury apartment complex. Countless restaurant and nightlife options abound nearby.

10 Belltown
MAP J4

Pedestrians are welcomed here with an explosion of stores, clubs, cafés, luxury condos, and fine restaurants. This upscale neighborhood was named after 1851 pioneer William N. Bell. In those days, the area attracted sailors on shore leave, artists seeking inexpensive loft spaces, and ragtag urban dwellers. However it was the dot-com boom of the 1990s that commercially revived the neighborhood. Remnants of old Belltown include some well-preserved facades.

DOWNTOWN SHOPPING SPREE

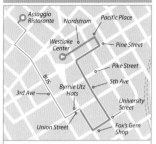

▶ MID-MORNING

Stop at **Westlake Center** (see p56) and grab an espresso and pastry at the stand in the plaza before window-shopping in Westlake's indoor mall. Inside, Made in Washington offers a large and creative inventory of regionally produced merchandise. Walk across Pine Street to find the spacious flagship **Nordstrom** store (see p56), stocked with top designer brands and the absolute best of everything. Stop at Nike Seattle (1500 6th Ave), where you can stock up on the latest trends in sportswear, then move on to splurge in **Pacific Place** mall (see p57), where customers can choose from upscale stores including Tiffany & Co., Coach, Ann Taylor, and Williams-Sonoma. Exit the mall on **Pine Street**, turn right, and then left on **5th Avenue** to **University Street** for pricey boutiques and fine jewelry, such as **Fox's Gem Shop** (1341 5th Ave).

Drop in for a quick cappuccino and a bite to eat to refuel at one of the many Starbucks shops, then go shopping for all-American headwear from **Byrnie Utz Hats** (see p76). Walk down **Union Street** to **3rd Avenue**, where you can board a number of non-express buses for a ride back to Pike Street, or, if you're feeling hungry, stay on the bus a few more blocks for a superb Italian lunch at **Assaggio Ristorante** (see p77) on 4th Avenue. Ask the driver for help if you need it.

See map on pp70–71

Around Belltown

The bar at The Big Picture theater

1 The Big Picture
MAP H3 ■ 2505 1st Ave ■ (206) 256-0566 ■ www.thebigpicture.net

An independent, first-run movie theater with a full bar. Entry is limited to those aged 21 and over.

2 Moore Theatre
MAP J4 ■ 1932 2nd Ave ■ (206) 682-1414 ■ www.stgpresents.org

This historic theater stages theatrical productions, concerts, and lectures.

3 Lenora Street Bridge
MAP H4

Leading from Western Avenue to the Elliott Bay piers, this elegant foot-bridge provides stellar views of West Seattle and the Olympic Mountains.

4 The Whisky Bar
MAP J4 ■ 2122 2nd Ave

This trendy bar in Belltown offers a large variety of whisky. It is good for pre-concert gatherings due to its proximity to the Moore Theatre.

5 Rendezvous/Jewel Box
MAP H3 ■ 2322 2nd Ave

Housing the minuscule Jewel Box Theater – a private movie-screening room built in 1926 – this remodeled bar attracts a hipster crowd (see p43).

6 Top Pot Doughnuts
MAP J3 ■ 2124 5th Ave

Take a break from healthy dining and grab a few doughnuts from this stylish café that welcomes loungers to sip the house-roasted coffee and dip the tasty homemade treats.

7 Sub Pop World Headquarters
MAP H3 ■ 2013 4th Ave

The local record label created by Jonathan Poneman and Bruce Pavitt in the mid-1980s has its headquarters here. They signed bands such as Nirvana and Soundgarden, putting Seattle on the rock music map.

8 Tula's Restaurant and Jazz Club
MAP J3 ■ 2214 2nd Ave ■ (206) 443-4221 ■ www.tulas.com

A mix of big names and well-known locals, and even high school jazz bands play here. Entry after 10pm is limited to those over the age of 21.

9 The Art Institute of Seattle
MAP H4 ■ 2323 Elliott Ave ■ (206) 448-6600

The institute offers a number of programs in design, fashion, media, and culinary arts. It also has an art gallery and a student-run restaurant.

10 Austin A. Bell Building
MAP H3 ■ 2326 1st Ave

Elmer Fisher, Seattle's foremost commercial architect, designed this building that reflects Richardsonian, Gothic, and Italianate styles. It houses pricey condos and a Starbucks.

Austin A. Bell Building facade

Belltown Shops

1 Brick + Mortar
MAP J4 ■ 1210 4th Ave (inside Fairmont Olympic Hotel) ■ (206) 588-2770 ■ www.brickmortarseattle.com

This men's shoe boutique specializes in Alden shoes and is licensed to design and custom-make a limited collection. Service is impeccable.

2 Vain
MAP J4 ■ 2018 1st Ave ■ (206) 441-3441 ■ www.vain.com

An innovative one-stop shop for hip consumers. Discover a full-service salon, an independent designer boutique, and an artists gallery.

3 Patagonia
MAP J4 ■ 2100 1st Ave ■ (206) 622-9700 ■ www.patagonia.com

The history of this purveyor of first-rate outdoor gear, rugged wear, and polar fleece comfort began with alpinist and founder Yvon Chouinard.

4 Robbins Brothers, The Engagement Ring Store
MAP J4 ■ 2200 1st Ave ■ (206) 336-1456

It would be hard to miss this store with the arty neon sign of a bejeweled ring glowing above it. Staff are well informed and easy-going.

5 Baby & Co.
MAP J4 ■ 1936 1st Ave ■ (206) 448-4077

The place to go for accessories for women, plus slacks, skirts, and dresses. Look for designs by Maria Calderara, Hannes Roether, Frank & Eileen, and Marithé and François Girbaud.

Purse from Baby & Co.

6 Karan Dannenberg Clothier
MAP J4 ■ 2232 1st Ave ■ (206) 453-6846

Original and elegant wear is offered for the sophisticated shopper, but expect the silk suits and lace-trimmed casuals to be expensive.

7 Endless Knot
MAP H3 ■ 2300 1st Ave ■ (206) 448-0355

Stocking sizes small to 3X, this shop sells artful designs with an Asian feel.

Sell Your Sole Consignment Boutique

8 Sell Your Sole Consignment Boutique
MAP J4 ■ 2121 1st Ave, suite 101 ■ (206) 443-2616 ■ www.sellyoursoleconsignment.com

Great service can be found at this women's clothing and shoes boutique, which stocks designer brands at up to 70 percent off their retail price. Look out for coveted labels such as McQueen, Chanel, Christian Louboutin, and Prada.

9 Sassafras
2307 1st Ave ■ (206) 7057 ■ www.sassafras-seattle.com

Inventive and beautifully crafted clothing and jewelry in a changing array of styles, designed and made by local artists. Gracious sales staff.

10 Moorea Seal
MAP J4 ■ 2523 3rd Ave ■ (206) 728-2523

An independent boutique featuring jewelry, gifts, and home decor items made by regional artists.

See map on pp70–71

Downtown Shops

(1) Pendleton
MAP K4 ■ 1313 4th Ave
■ www.pendleton-usa.com

In 1863, British weaver Thomas Kay founded the Pendleton woolen company, which specializes in blankets and clothes for men and women.

(2) Byrnie Utz Hats
MAP K4 ■ 310 Union St
■ (206) 623-0233 ■ www.byrnieutz.com

With a store in this location since 1934, Bernie Utz sells cowboy hats, newsy caps, and everything in between.

Hat for sale, Byrnie Utz Hats

(3) AllSaints
MAP K4 ■ 1511 5th Ave & Pine ■ (206) 508-0018 ■ www.us.allsaints.com

Trendy British clothing brand for women and men. Urban style and cutting-edge designs are echoed in the warehouse-style store.

(4) Metsker Maps of Seattle
MAP J4 ■ 1511 1st Ave ■ (206) 623-8747 ■ www.metskers.com

Geography enthusiasts will lose themselves in this impressive store, where customers can peruse and buy a variety of maps, travel guides, moon charts, and globes.

(5) Paper Hammer
MAP J4 ■ 1400 2nd Ave ■ (206) 682-3820 ■ www.paper-hammer.com

This quirky store sells letter-press arts and stationery, limited-run postcards, and notebooks.

(6) Bella Umbrella
MAP J4 ■ 1535 1st Ave ■ (206) 297-1540 ■ www.bellaumbrella.com

To combat Seattle's notoriously rainy weather, invest in one of the top-notch umbrellas that are rented and sold at this friendly store. All shapes, sizes, and colors are available, from fashion and golf umbrellas to high-tech models and parasols.

(7) Fireworks
MAP K4
■ Westlake Center, 400 Pine St ■ (206) 682-6462 ■ www.fireworksgallery.net

Shop here for handmade tableware, jewelry, clothing, whimsical books, and toys for the kids. There is a store at the airport, too, for that last-minute gift.

(8) Isadoras Antique Jewelry
MAP J4 ■ 1601 1st Ave ■ (206) 441 7711 ■ www.isadoras.com

Offering new, designer, vintage, and private-label pieces, Isadora's collection of estate jewelry has been a hit since it opened in the late 1970s. There are lots of incredible finds.

(9) John Fluevog Shoes
MAP K4 ■ 205 Pine St ■ (206) 441-1065 ■ www.fluevog.com

High style and comfort are combined in John Fluevog's quirky designs. Prices are surprisingly affordable, and twice-yearly sales in January and July offer excellent value.

(10) Mariners Team Store
MAP J4 ■ 1800 4th Ave ■ (206) 346-4327 ■ www.mlbshop.com

For those who want to fit in, this is the place to purchase official team jerseys and T-shirts, baseball caps, and other gift items emblazoned with the Mariners' – Seattle's winning professional league team – logo.

Paper Hammer stationery store

Belltown Places to Eat

PRICE CATEGORIES

Price categories include a three-course meal for one, two glasses of wine, and all unavoidable extra charges including tax.

$ under $40 $$ $40–80 $$$ over $80

1 Cyclops
MAP H3 ■ 2421 1st Ave
■ (206) 441-1677 ■ $

Interview and Details magazines have raved about this place, and local customers keep returning to enjoy a classic hummus plate.

2 Assaggio Ristorante
MAP J3 ■ 2010 4th Ave
■ (206) 441-1399 ■ $$$

Savor tasty authentic Italian cuisine such as *pappardelle cinghiale* (pasta ribbons with wild boar sauce) and *osso buco*. Many of the desserts, such as tiramisu, are imported from Italy.

3 Dahlia Lounge
MAP J3 ■ 2001 4th Ave
■ (206) 682-4142 ■ $$

This restaurant serves organic, local food with an Asian flavor, and is known for its coconut cream pie *(see p54)*.

4 Queen City Grill
MAP J4 ■ 2201 1st Ave
■ (206) 443-0975 ■ $$

Ideal for a romantic meal, this place offers a softly lit dining room, superb cocktails, delicious dishes such as grilled fish or lamb, and live jazz.

5 Mama's Cantina
MAP J3 ■ 2234 2nd Ave
■ (206) 728-6262 ■ $

Huge portions of Mexican classics (burritos, tacos, enchiladas) and strong margaritas are served in a noisy and festive environment.

6 Macrina Bakery & Café
MAP H3 ■ 2408 1st Ave
■ (206) 448-4032 ■ $

A cherished bakery café famous for its bread pudding with fresh cream and berries, salads, and sandwiches.

7 Local 360
MAP H3 ■ 2234 1st Ave
■ (206) 441-9360 ■ $

A community-minded restaurant that sources ingredients from farmers within a 360-mile (579-km) radius. Expect a casual, eclectic crowd.

Entrance to El Gaucho steakhouse

8 El Gaucho
MAP H3 ■ 2505 1st Ave
■ (206) 728-1337 ■ $$

One of Seattle's premier steakhouses, where diners flock to order from an extensive menu featuring 28-day, dry-aged Angus prime beef, fresh seafood, and delicious side orders.

9 Two Bells Bar & Grill
MAP J3 ■ 2313 4th Ave
■ (206) 441-3050 ■ $

This eatery served great pub grub, especially burgers, with microbrews on tap. There is occasional live music.

10 Belltown Pizza
MAP H3 ■ 2422 1st Ave
■ (206) 441-2653 ■ $

With a neighborhood bar atmosphere, this pizzeria offers a number of both standard and gourmet New-York style pizzas, which can be ordered by the slice. There is also a small pasta selection – try the gorgonzola-and-walnut-stuffed ravioli.

See map on pp70–71

🔟 Capitol Hill

Discover one of Seattle's most electrifying neighborhoods on the long ridge that stretches northeast of downtown. The large gay, lesbian, and transgender resident population helped to create a vibrant culture reflected in street scenes that hover on the outside edge of mainstream society. There may be more dyed and spiked hair and imaginatively applied body piercings here than elsewhere in Seattle, but Capitol Hill is much more than a magnet for self-expression. Abundant stores, clubs, restaurants, and cafés along Broadway, Pike and Pine Streets, and 15th Avenue East attract crowds from all over the city. Key attractions include two vintage movie theaters – the Harvard Exit and the Egyptian Theater – the Cornish College of the Arts, the Central Seattle Community College, and the Seattle Asian Art Museum in the sylvan setting of Volunteer Park.

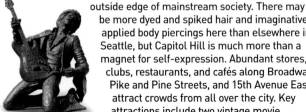

Jimi Hendrix Statue

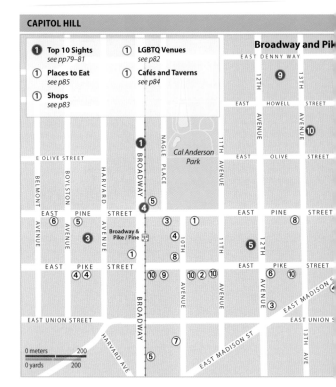

CAPITOL HILL

- ① **Top 10 Sights** see pp79–81
- ① **Places to Eat** see p85
- ① **Shops** see p83
- ① **LGBTQ Venues** see p82
- ① **Cafés and Taverns** see p84

Inside Unicorn Bar, Broadway

1 Broadway

If it can be bought, it can be found on Broadway, the nerve center of Capitol Hill *(see pp24–5)*. From East Pike to East Roy Streets, store-fronts beckon consumers on the hunt for food, vintage and new cloth-ing, vinyl records, and lots of coffee.

On summer evenings especially, the density of pedestrian traffic along Broadway almost matches that of midtown Manhattan.

2 East Capitol Hill
MAP E4

The area around 19th Avenue has its own restaurant scene – Hello Robin serves milk and carefully made cookies next to Molly Moon's Home-made Ice Cream take-out window. Cone & Steiner has a gourmet deli, and Fuel Coffee is a popular local hangout. There is a fountain plaza at Miller Community Center and the streets are lined with turn-of-the-century homes. A little farther north, there is cozy Volunteer Park Café.

3 Pike/Pine Corridor
MAP E4

Bisecting Capitol Hill are two busy streets offering their own flavor and subculture. You can find many of the area's gay and lesbian hangouts on the blocks above and below Broadway, as well as a great selec-tion of taverns and stores selling vintage housewares and furnishings. Although the city has tried to dis-courage their postings, you may also notice colorful flyers stapled onto telephone poles and virtually any surface, advertising band concerts in the vicinity. If nothing else, they draw attention to the pulse that keeps this community living and breathing.

Posters on the Pike/Pine Corridor

4 Jimi Hendrix Statue

Daryl Smith, an artist once based at the Fremont Fine Arts Foundry, created a lifesized bronze statue of Jimi Hendrix that now graces the Pine Street sidewalk. It shows the musician in his trademark rockstar pose, kneeling in bell-bottoms with his Fender guitar pointed skyward. Before Paul Allen founded the Museum of Pop Culture (see p40), which was inspired by Hendrix and his music, this installation was the best-known memorial dedicated to the guitarist (see p25).

5 Northwest Film Forum

MAP M3 ▪ 1515 12th Ave ▪ (206) 329-2629 ▪ www.nwfilm forum.org

This festival screens more than 200 independent films every year in its two theaters, which are equipped with top-of-the-range sound and projection gear. The Forum also hosts events all year round, including talks by visiting directors and actors, and workshops for aspiring film-makers. It also acts as a venue for other festivals – like the Three Dollar Bill Cinema LGBTQ film festival.

Volunteer Park Water Tower

6 Volunteer Park Water Tower

MAP M1 ▪ Open 6am–10pm daily

Built by Seattle's water department in 1906, this 75-ft- (23-m-) tall brick tower with an observation deck was designed by the Olmsted Brothers. A short climb of 107 spiraling steps to the deck offers spectacular views of Puget Sound, the Space Needle, and the Olympic Mountains. Volunteer Park (see p46) is also the site of the Seattle Asian Art Museum (see p38) and the Volunteer Park Conservatory.

7 LGBTQ Scene

Gay and lesbian clubs (see p82) proliferate on the Hill, as do adult stores selling costumes and accessories.

8 Lake View Cemetery

MAP E3 ▪ 1554 15th E ▪ (206) 322-1582 ▪ www.lakeview cemeteryassociation.com

This 1872-era cemetery, sitting on a hilltop just past the northern end of Volunteer Park, is the final resting place for prominent Seattleites. Tombstones here identify the city's pioneers whose names now grace present-day streets or area towns – Denny, Maynard, Boren, Mercer, Yesler, and Renton are some examples. Lake View Cemetery also draws the faithful followers of cinema star and martial arts master Bruce Lee (see p37) and his son, whose sculpted tombstones lie side by side.

SEATTLE PRIDE MARCH

What began as a protest in 1970 to commemorate the first anniversary of the Stonewall Riots in New York (which sparked the gay rights movement) has become a day of celebration, music, and pageantry. Although Capitol Hill can no longer accommodate the large numbers that come to participate – the rally now takes place in Seattle Center (below) – the Hill remains important for Seattle's gay community.

9 Neighborhood Homes
Stroll down the three-block stretch of Denny between Broadway and Olive Way to scout for charming Victorian and Craftsman-style homes and elegant balconies decorated with hanging flower baskets or offbeat art. Marvel at the opulent mansions on the blocks just south of Volunteer Park. Capitol Hill's adjacent Central District, south of Madison and north of 14th Avenue East, is a transitional neighborhood with gorgeous homes.

10 Cathedrals
St. Nicholas Russian Orthodox Cathedral: MAP M3; 1714 13th Ave ■ St. Mark's Episcopal Cathedral: MAP E4; 1245 10th Ave E

Capitol Hill has numerous landmark places of worship, including the grand St. Mark's Episcopal Cathedral, which belongs to the Diocese of Olympia. Organ enthusiasts come from afar to play the 3,944-pipe Flentrop organ. St. Nicholas Russian Orthodox Cathedral, one of the oldest parishes of the Russian Orthodox Church outside Russia, was founded in 1930 by immigrants who fled the 1917 Russian Revolution. The structure's ornate turquoise *lukovitsa* (16th-century "onion dome" style of cupolas) and spires rise high above the trees and neighboring homes.

St. Mark's Episcopal Cathedral nave

UP PINE DOWN PIKE

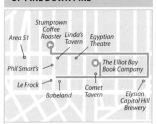

▶ MORNING

Begin your late morning walk at the corner of Pine and Boylston with a strong coffee at **Stumptown Coffee Roasters** (616 Pine St). Walk along Pine (slightly uphill toward Broadway), but make a detour to check out **Le Frock Vintage** (613 E Pike St) for its selection of vintage and new consignment clothing, or stop at **Area 51** (401 E Pine St), a huge space filled with vintage furniture and kitschy one-of-a-kinds. One block farther east lies **Linda's Tavern** (see p84), a legendary local watering hole frequented by musicians and record label folk, which can be scoped out for a later visit. Cross Harvard Avenue and look out for the vintage **Egyptian Theatre** (see p43) on the right, which showcases independent and foreign films.

AFTERNOON

Cross Broadway, walk for four blocks, and turn right on 13th Avenue to Pike Street. Turn right and have lunch at **Elysian Capitol Hill Public Brewery** (see p84), home of Seattle's most outstanding pale ale. Walk downhill on Pike to the **Comet Tavern** (see p84), a grungy place that is popular with local musicians and wannabes. Cross Broadway and dream about purchasing a gold-trimmed imported sports car at Ferrari of Seattle (1401 12th Ave), or stop by **Babeland** (see p82), a store selling a variety of adult toys. Then grab a cup of coffee and a snack and get lost in the stacks of one of the city's most popular bookstores, **The Elliott Bay Book Company** (see p24).

See map on pp78–9

LGBTQ Venues

 Neighbours
MAP M3 ▪ 1509 Broadway

Witness hedonism at its best, with talent shows, wet 'n' wild contests, open mike nights, album launch parties, nightly drink specials, and dancing boys. Thursdays through Saturdays the club stays open late.

 Re-bar
MAP L3 ▪ 1114 Howell St

This dive bar has high-spirited live acts on stage, including some of the area's best DJs, and is great for a fun night of dancing. The entrance sign sums up its philosophy – "no minors, drunks, drugs, bigots, or loud-mouths."

Entrance to Re-bar nightclub

 LGBTQ Visitors Center
MAP M2 ▪ 614 Broadway E
▪ (206) 363-9188 ▪ www.thegsba.org/travel-gay-seattle

Located inside 1st Security Bank, this center has tellers that are trained to help LGBTQ visitors with the answers to all their questions.

4 **Babeland**
MAP L3 ▪ 707 E Pike St
▪ (206) 328-2914

Primarily a store selling sex toys, this spot also sponsors sex workshops that both amuse and shock.

 The Crescent Lounge
MAP L3 ▪ 1413 E Olive Way
▪ (206) 720-8188

This local dive bar is the current trendy hipster hangout for the LGBTQ crowd, with entertaining karaoke and reasonably priced drinks.

 R Place
MAP L3 ▪ 619 E Pine St

Capitol Hill's largest gay club has something for everyone. There is a full bar and music video monitors on the first floor; dartboards, free pool, and pinball on the second floor; and dancing, live DJs, karaoke, and a weekly strip show on the third floor.

 Eagle
MAP L3 ▪ 314 E Pike St

This is Seattle's oldest leather bar, and the atmosphere reeks of a crowd driven by studs, black leather straps and hard rock music.

 The Cuff Complex
MAP M3 ▪ 1533 13th Ave

An exclusive gay men's bar and dance complex catering for a crowd ranging from 20-somethings to the middle-aged. Arrive on Sundays for a kegger blowout.

9 **Diesel Seattle**
MAP M3 ▪ 1413 14th Ave
▪ (206) 322-1080

Visitors can count on a fun and friendly crowd (and plenty of leather) at one of the city's oldest gay bars. Drinks are generous and bar food plentiful. Taco Tuesdays are hugely popular.

 Wildrose
MAP M3 ▪ 1021 E Pike St

One of the oldest lesbian bars on the West Coast, this place does not encourage many solo male guests. However, many couples do visit the club for the dancing, the strong drinks, and the karaoke. Poetry readings, open mike nights, and pool tournaments add to the action.

Shops

Racks of colorful second-hand clothes for sale at Pretty Parlor

1 **Pretty Parlor**
MAP L2 ■ 119 Summit Ave E
■ (206) 405-2883 ■ www.pretty
parlor.com
Stocked full with vintage and indie clothing for women, this store is the place to find a unique wardrobe item.

2 **Martin-Zambito Gallery**
MAP L4 ■ 1117 Minor Ave
■ (206) 726-9509
Established in 1986, this art gallery specializes in 19th- to 21st-century American and early Northwest Regionalism, with special emphasis put on contemporary figurative art, and early women artists.

3 **Fleet Feet Sports**
MAP L3 ■ 911 E Pine St
■ www.fleetfeetseattle.com
This store stocks dozens of top brands. The knowledgeable staff can fit even the most finicky sports lovers with proper accessories.

4 **The Elliott Bay Book Company**
Peruse the huge selection at this excellent independent bookstore and Seattle institution *(see p24)*. It also has its own café, Little Oddfellows.

5 **Sugar Pill Apothecary**
MAP M3 ■ 900 E Pine St ■ (206) 322-7455 ■ www.sugarpillseattle.com
Much of the inventory at this quirky store is produced by women-owned businesses. Organic chocolates, spa goods, and spices are some of the items sold here.

6 **Wall of Sound**
MAP L3 ■ 1205 E Pike St
A treasured, small, independent shop selling new and rare CDs and LPs. Wall of Sound carries obscure recordings of rock, jazz, ethnic, electronic, and modern classical, and anything out of the ordinary.

7 **KOBO**
MAP L3 ■ 814 E Roy St ■ (206) 726-0704 ■ www.koboseattle.com
An elegant, tightly curated gallery of art and quality jewelry, home goods, gifts, and crafts from Japanese and Pacific Northwest artisans.

8 **Cone & Steiner**
MAP F4 ■ 532 19th Ave E ■ (206) 582-1928 ■ coneandsteiner.com
This gourmet neighborhood market has wine and chocolate tastings and a top-quality take-out deli.

9 **Quest Bookshop**
MAP L3 ■ 717 Broadway Ave E
■ (206) 323-4281 ■ www.quest
books.com
As well as more than 11,000 titles covering religion, mysticism, and spiritualism, Quest offers personal astrological charts and tarot decks.

10 **Retail Therapy**
MAP M3 ■ 905 E Pike St ■ (206) 324-4092 ■ www.ineedretailtherapy.com
This store sells clothing, small-batch fragrances, gifts, jewelry, art, and accessories made by independent artists and designers.

See map on pp78–9

Cafés and Taverns

Exposed brickwork and trendy lighting in Victrola Coffee Roasters

1 Victrola Coffee Roasters
MAP E4 ■ 411 15th Ave E ■ $

A real neighborhood café that prides itself on roasting its own coffee in-house, using beans from small farms.

2 Caffé Vita
MAP M3 ■ 1005 E Pike St ■ (206) 709-4440 ■ $

Dark walls and ceilings, wooden floors, and excellent coffee set the tone here. It roasts its own coffee; look through the back window to see the apparatus.

3 Tavern Law
MAP M3 ■ 1406 12th Ave ■ (206) 322-9734 ■ $

A hip, stylish, speakeasy-style lounge, offering well-made cocktails and thoughtful comfort fare to young professionals looking to unwind.

4 Chop Suey
MAP E4 ■ 1325 E Madison St ■ (206) 324-8005 ■ $

Go for the hip-hop on Sundays and local hard rock bands the rest of the week (see p52).

5 Linda's Tavern
MAP L3 ■ 707 E Pine St ■ (206) 325-1220 ■ $

Linda Derschang, a local business owner, created a hip bar for locals in 1994 (who tended to be rock stars). Drinks and decent food are on offer.

6 Hopvine Pub
MAP E4 ■ 507 15th Ave E ■ (206) 328-3120 ■ $

This neighborhood bar serves tasty pub fare and good handcrafted cask ales from small breweries.

7 Cederberg Tea House
MAP G1 ■ 1417 Queen Anne Ave N, 101B ■ (206) 285-1352 ■ $$

This elegant South African Tea House offers dozens of exotic teas as well as freshly baked sweet and savory snacks. Try the Malva pudding.

8 Comet Tavern
MAP M3 ■ 922 E Pike St ■ $

A legendary hangout for rockers and great pretenders alike. This is just a normal tavern with some pool tables, but the crowd tells a different tale.

9 Fuel Coffee
MAP F4 ■ 610 19th Ave E ■ (206) 329-4700 ■ www.fuelcoffee seattle.com ■ $

This cozy local café serves strong espresso and treats from High 5 Pie. The walls feature local art.

10 Elysian Brewing Company
MAP M3 ■ 1221 E Pike St ■ (206) 860-1920 ■ $

The food here rates among some of the best pub grub in town (see p53).

Places to Eat

PRICE CATEGORIES
Price categories include a three-course meal for one, two glasses of wine, and all unavoidable extra charges including tax.

$ under $40 $$ $40–80 $$$ over $80

1 Rancho Bravo Tacos
MAP M4 ▪ 1001 E Pine St
▪ (206) 322-9399 ▪ $

A colorful, no-frills taqueria, with friendly, attentive staff. Loyal customers love the affordable plates of fresh, authentic Mexican fare.

2 DeLuxe Bar & Grill
MAP M1 ▪ 625 Broadway E
▪ (206) 324-9697 ▪ $

Serves an enviable list of brews and better-than-usual pub fare including nachos, burgers, and salads.

3 Aoki
MAP M1 ▪ 621 Broadway E
▪ (206) 324-3633 ▪ $

A longtime Broadway establishment, Aoki rivals any sushi restaurant in town. Sit at the bar to watch the food being prepared.

4 Honey Hole
MAP L3 ▪ 703 E Pike St
▪ (206) 709-1399 ▪ $

Find your way to this heartwarming source of Capitol Hill's biggest and most succulent sandwiches.

5 Garage
MAP M4 ▪ 1130 Broadway ▪ (206) 322-2296 ▪ $

Dodge the crowds at this fine dining, drinking, pool, and bowling spot.

Garage diner

6 Terra Plata
MAP L3 ▪ 1501 Melrose Ave
▪ (206) 325-1501 ▪ $$$

This restaurant serves bistro-style plates with a focus on local produce. The rooftop patio is the place to be.

7 Lark
MAP M4 ▪ 952 E Seneca St
▪ (206) 323-5275 ▪ www.larkseattle. com ▪ $$

An upscale bistro with big sharing plates of Northwest cuisine (see p54).

8 Annapurna Café
MAP M3 ▪ 1833 Broadway
▪ (206) 320-7770 ▪ No wheelchair access ▪ $

This restaurant puts Nepalese, Indian, and Tibetan cuisine under one roof. Choose from dumplings, tandoori dishes, or curry items.

9 Via Tribunali
MAP L3 ▪ 913 E Pike St
▪ (206) 322-9234 ▪ $$

Some of the best authentic Italian pizza in town, with generous, delicious toppings and excellent crusts.

10 Quinn's Pub
MAP L3 ▪ 1001 E Pike St
▪ (206) 325-7711 ▪ $

A popular, upscale bar where guests dine on gourmet burgers and modern American comfort fare. The wild boar Sloppy Joe and house-made sausage with lentils are popular.

🔟 Fremont

Fremont declared itself an "artists' republic" in the 1960s, when a community of students, artists, and bohemians moved in, attracted by low rents. The name crystallizes the unflagging spirit of independence, eccentricity, and nonconformity here. In retrospect, what may have begun as an idealistic artists' enclave was more accurately an early sign of gentrification. The scenic Lake Washington Ship Canal and part of Lake Union create its southern border, and passing boats continually refresh the view. The drawbridge on busy Fremont Avenue rises and falls many times a day, and heavy traffic backs up the hill. The quaint neighborhood spawns new boutiques, clubs, and restaurants that keep changing the identity of this town. As Seattle grows, more people seek homes here, only minutes away from downtown.

Art Nouveau lamp, Fremont Market

FREMONT

1 Top 10 Sights
see pp89–91

1 Places to Eat
see p95

1 Shops
see p94

1 Burke-Gilman Trail Features
see p93

1 Fremont Culture
see p92

See inset map right

Central Fremont

Previous pages View of the skyscrapers along the Seattle Waterfront

1 Lenin Statue
MAP D2 ▪ **3526 Fremont Ave N**

Slovakian sculptor Emil Venkov (1937–2017) found little interest in his 7-ton (6,350-kg), 25-ft- (8-m-) tall likeness of Russian revolutionary Vladimir Lenin after the collapse of the Soviet Union. A visiting American, Lewis Carpenter, paid $13,000 for the work and had it shipped through the Panama Canal to his hometown near Seattle. After Carpenter died in 1994, Fremont artist and foundry owner Peter Bevis managed to have the bronze Lenin statue installed in the neighborhood. The incongruity of a Communist icon amidst flourishing shops and capitalist businesses is not lost on anyone. Even so, the statue remains a striking symbol that strives to put art before politics.

Fremont Troll under Aurora Bridge

2 Fremont Troll
MAP D2 ▪ **Intersection of Aurora Ave (Hwy 99) & N 36th St**

An icon of Fremont's free spirit is a 15-ft- (4.5-m-) tall troll created by Steve Badanes, Will Martin, Donna Walter, and Ross Whitehead, after a national competition sponsored by the Fremont Arts Council (see p92). In 1989, the council decided that public art was the best use for a dark space beneath a highway bridge. The troll's location under the north end of Aurora Bridge means that it features on almost every tour.

3 Fremont Bridge
MAP D3 ▪ **3020 Westlake Ave N**

The lowest of four bridges spanning the Lake Washington Ship Canal, Fremont Bridge connects Fremont to residential Queen Anne and two main arterials to downtown. Due to the bridge's low clearance, it faces frequent openings from passing vessels. Neon art adorns a portion of the span, in the form of a blonde Rapunzel with her hair cascading from a tower's window.

Fremont Bridge

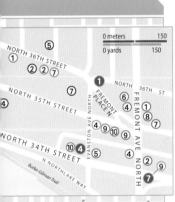

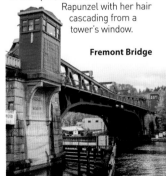

4 Sunday Street Market

MAP D2 ■ 34th St ■ (206) 781-6776 ■ Every Sunday ■ Open Apr–Oct: 10am–5pm; Nov–Mar: 10am–4pm ■ www.fremontmarket.com

The Fremont Sunday Market has withstood the test of time, real estate development, and even lawsuits from neighboring businesses. Begun in 1990 to foster a pedestrian-friendly community and provide an outlet for artists and independent vendors to sell their wares, the market hosts up to 200 booths of crafts, imported goods, furniture, food, and knick-knacks that defy description.

5 Dinosaur Topiaries

MAP D2 ■ Intersection of Phinney Ave & 34th St

Two ivy-covered dinosaur topiaries, which had formerly decorated the lawn near the Pacific Science Center (see p15) at Seattle Center, now grace Fremont's narrow Ship Canal Park. To save them from extinction, History House and a group of Fremont artists purchased them in 1999 for $1. The 66-ft- (20-m-) long mother and the young *apatosauri* are now sanctioned by the city and fully integrated into a neighborhood-wide sculpture garden.

6 Fremont Canal Park

MAP C2 ■ Phinney Ave & 2nd Ave NW

A lovely landscaped strip – not a great deal wider than a stretch of

Waiting for the Interurban **sculpture**

Waterfront path, Fremont Canal Park

the Burke-Gilman Trail (see p93) – attracts tourists all year round. The park creates viewpoints along the canal and offers several places to sit, play chess, enjoy a picnic, and watch the world go by. Pedestrians do not need to dodge speeding bicycles, however, since there is a separate cycle path.

7 Waiting for the Interurban

MAP D2 ■ N 34th St & Fremont Ave N

Frozen in time, artist Richard Beyer's celebrated 1979 cast aluminum sculpture – five human forms and a dog with a human face – presides at Fremont's busiest road intersection, where a community trolley once stopped. Legend has it that the dog's likeness belongs to Arman Napoleon Stepanian, an activist-hero who sparked the recycling movement some 30 years ago. The work pokes fun at modern humanity's ennui. It also represents one of Seattle's earliest public art installations.

8 Fremont Ferry and Sunday Ice Cream Cruise

MAP D3 ■ (206) 713-8446 ■ Sunday Ice Cream Cruise: 11am–4pm all year round ■ Adm ■ www.seattleferry service.com

A labor of love for Captain Larry Kezner, this passenger-only ferry plies the waters of Lake Union from the north shore in Fremont to Lake Union Park on the south shore just four times a year. For a more regular boat service, the Sunday Ice Cream Cruise departs every Sunday on the hour from Lake Union Park.

9 Fremont Brewing Company

MAP D2 ■ 1050 N 34th St. ■ (206) 420-2407

This kid and dog-friendly "urban beer garden" has become a neighborhood hub for all ages. It specialises in microbrews made with local ingredients, and in promoting community causes and events.

Entrance to the History House

10 History House

MAP D2 ■ 900 N 34th St ■ (206) 675-8875 ■ Adm (donation) ■ www.historyhouse.org

Seattle's colorful past can be viewed at History House, where historians preserve the heritage of the city's distinct neighborhoods. A three-sided sepia-tone wall mural depicts over 100 years of Seattle history in the arts, technology, and industry. Browse rotating displays of various Seattle neighborhoods. Other features here include a sculpture garden and a gift shop. Call for opening hours, as renovations are in progress.

A MORNING AROUND FREMONT

▶ MORNING

Start the day with an espresso at **Espresso To Go** *(3512 Fremont Place N)*. Take the crosswalk just outside the door to 35th Street, turning right to spy the neon-adorned Army surplus missile known as the **Rocket**. Turn left on Evanston and walk a block to **PCC Natural Markets** *(600 N 34th St)*, an organic food market, to pick up a delicious carry-out lunch.

Turn left on Evanston for an unobstructed view of the **Fremont Cut** and **Fremont Bridge** *(see p89)*. Turn right along the Canal path, walk about a block until you see the **Dinosaur Topiaries** at the entrance to the **Fremont Canal Park** – a great place to enjoy a waterfront picnic. The **Old Trolley Barn** *(see p93)* is a historic brick building that now houses **Theo Chocolate** *(see p92)*, a gourmet chocolate factory. Enjoy the walk down the canal path, spotting sailboats or kayakers. When turning back, exit the park at the topiaries and continue along 34th Street. During the Sunday Street Market, there will be blocks of vendors here. Continue three blocks to Fremont Avenue, by the Fremont Bridge and the sculpture, *Waiting for the Interurban*, on a traffic island across the street. Turn left on Fremont Avenue, and get your bearings at the **Center of the Universe signpost**, which is a half-block later on another traffic island where Fremont Place begins. Stop in **Simply Desserts** *(3421 Fremont Ave N)* for some of the richest treats in town.

See map on pp88–9

Fremont Culture

Parade performers, Fremont Fair

1 Fremont Fair

The Solstice Parade *(see p60)*, which includes colorfully clad participants, people-powered floats, and even naked cyclists, kicks off this fair with food, crafts, and music.

2 First Fridays Art Walk

■ Fremont Foundry's Gallery 154: MAP C2; 154 N 35th

On the first Friday of each month, galleries organize self-guided art walks to local studios and establishments, including the Fremont Foundry's Gallery and the Fremont Coffee Company *(see p55)*.

3 Trolloween

MAP D2 ■ 36th St N under Aurora Ave

A lively parade that begins its route near the Fremont Troll *(see p89)*, this takeoff on Halloween ends at a bizarre masked ball with light shows and live entertainment.

4 Theo Chocolate

MAP D2 ■ 3400 Phinney Ave N ■ (206) 632-5100 ■ www. theochocolate.com

Visitors can see chocolate being made and can feast on samples at the country's first organic, fair trade chocolate company. It sources its beans from all over the world.

5 The Backdoor at Roxy's

MAP C2 ■ 462 N 36th St ■ (206) 632-7322 ■ www.backdooratroxys.com

This speakeasy lounge has an edgy, baroque-style decor. Go for the Ryan Gosling cocktail and Fremont fries.

6 Fremont Arts Council

MAP D2 ■ 3940 Fremont Ave N ■ (206) 547-7440 ■ www.fremontarts council.org

Based in an elementary school's 1892-vintage powerhouse, this community organization supports artists and creative expression.

7 Glass Art

Edge of Glass: MAP D2; 513 N 36th St; (206) 632-7807; www. edgeofglass.com

Local artist Dale Chihuly's *(see p39)* influence can be seen in glass studios such as Edge of Glass.

8 Moisture Festival

MAP C2 ■ 4301 Leary Way NW ■ www.moisturefestival.com

This addition to the funky Fremont scene combines elements of burlesque and carnival for two weeks in spring. It is held at the old Hale's Ales Brewery.

9 Pumpkin-Carving Contests

www.fremontoktoberfest. com

During the Oktoberfest celebrations – Fremont's beer festival – hilarious chainsaw pumpkin-carving competitions take place on the stage.

Lily Verlaine, Moisture Festival

10 Fremont Library

MAP D2 ■ 731 N 35th St ■ (206) 684-4084

The city's most charming library attracts resident literati who spend hours here instead of buying the latest author's masterpiece online.

Burke-Gilman Trail Features

1 Lake Washington Rowing Club
MAP D3 ▪ 910 N Northlake Way

Both the local athletic teams and amateur rowers hoist their boats into the river from here. The club's nonprofit activities also include training lessons for beginners.

2 Old Trolley Barn
MAP D2 ▪ 34th & Phinney Ave N

This large brick warehouse used to house Seattle's early mass transit vehicles – the trolleys. Since then, the building has been, among other things, a microbrewery, and is now home to the Theo Chocolate store.

3 Dock Overlook
MAP C2

This fenced-in area with benches and a roof sits right on the water, making it perfect for watching birds, boats and sunsets. Far-reaching views include Salmon Bay's dry-dock industry and the vast Olympic Mountains beyond to the west.

4 The Rocket
MAP D2 ▪ 35th & Evanston Ave N

When an Army surplus store closed in Belltown, its outside adornment ended up in the hands of a group of Fremont sculptors and painters who renovated the World War II-era missile and placed it here, atop the Burnt Sugar shoe store.

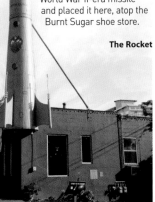

The Rocket

5 Bridges

The Burke-Gilman Trail makes its way under the Fremont Bridge (see p89) and the Aurora Bridge. Both span the Ship Canal, although only the drawbridge opens for boat traffic.

Aurora Bridge and the trail below

6 Rope Swing
MAP D2

Sunny summer days attract a crowd of rope-swingers who get dunked in the canal near Phinney Ave N.

7 Adobe Systems
MAP D3 ▪ 801 N 34th St ▪ (206) 675-7000

A waterfront office building, which was designed to imitate the look of Fremont's erstwhile industrial structures, houses this software company.

8 Indoor Sun Shoppe
MAP C2 ▪ 160 N Canal St

Huge, exotic plants decorate the shopfront of Seattle's favorite neighborhood home and garden store.

9 Waiting for the Interurban

This is one of the city's first public art installations, and makes a great backdrop for a group photo (see p90).

10 Gravel Plant
MAP C2

The mounds of gravel and asphalt here create a stark contrast to the serenity of the parkland nearby.

See map on pp88–9

Shops

Browsing vinyls at Jive Time Records

Les Amis
5 MAP D2 = 3420 Evanston Ave N = (206) 632-2877 = www.lesamis-inc.com

Window-shoppers find it hard to resist the rustic charm of this women's boutique that stocks designer items by Rozae Nichols, Isabel Marant, and AG Jeans.

Frame Up Studios
6 MAP D2 = 3515 Fremont Ave N = (206) 547-4657 = www.frameupstudios.com

A simple framing shop that turned itself into a lovely and sophisticated resource for one-of-a-kind gift items.

Jive Time Records
1 MAP D2 = 3506 Fremont Ave N = (206) 632-5483 = www.jivetimerecords.com

Discover quality vintage jazz, hip-hop, and electronic albums – no music obsessions are too obscure here, and there are heaps of vinyls to be found.

Dusty Strings
2 MAP D2 = 3406 Fremont Ave N = (206) 634-1662 = www.dustystrings.com

Since 1979, this store has attracted players and fans of folk music looking for a levered harp, fiddle, acoustic guitar, or a workshop on dulcimers.

evo
3 MAP D2 = 3500 Stone Way N = (206) 973-4470 = www.alltogetherskatepark.com

This sporting goods store sells an array of outdoor gear – everything from skis to skateboards. It is located in the Fremont Collective, which is also home to the All Together Skatepark (ATS), the city's only indoor skatepark.

Bellefleur Lingerie Boutique
4 MAP D2 = 3504 Fremont Pl N = (206) 545-0222 = www.bellefleurlingerie.com

This lingerie boutique caters for brides and anyone else who wants to indulge in some luxury.

Show Pony
7 MAP D2 = 702 N 35th St = (206) 706-4188 = www.showponyboutique.com

This well-curated boutique stocks everything from vintage consignment fashions to clothing, jewelry, and accessories by local designers.

Ophelia's Books
8 MAP C2 = 3504 Fremont Ave N = (206) 632-3759 = www.opheliasbooks.com

There are three floors of new and used books here, with a large selection of rare and out-of-print editions.

Fremont Vintage Mall
9 MAP D2 = 3419 Fremont Place N = (206) 548-9140

This underground warren features vintage clothing, furniture, and records, among other treasures.

Essenza Inc
10 MAP D2 = 615 N 35th St = (206) 547-4895 = www.essenza-inc.com

A funky shop, Essenza Inc sells a well-chosen assortment of cosmetics, perfumes, bath and skincare products, jewelry, and women's lingerie.

See map on p88–9

Places to Eat

PRICE CATEGORIES
Price categories include a three-course meal for one, two glasses of wine, and all unavoidable extra charges including tax.

$ under $40 $$ $40–80 $$$ over $80

1 Revel
MAP D2 ■ 403 N 36th S
■ (206) 547-2040 ■ $$$

Tuck into Korean fusion cuisine in this casual space with its pleasant outdoor patio. The rice bowls and ramen are famously good. If there is a wait, have a *soju* (rice liquor) or Asian-inspired cocktail in the adjoining bar until a table is ready.

2 Kwanjai Thai Cuisine
MAP D2 ■ 469 N 36th St
■ (206) 632-3656 ■ $

It is hard to go wrong when ordering off the specials board or the regular menu in this Thai restaurant.

3 Tacos Guaymas
MAP C2 ■ 100 N 36th
■ (206) 547-5110 ■ $

This Mexican restaurant offers freshly prepared traditional dishes such as *chile rellenos*, quesadillas, tacos, and burritos. There is also a salsa bar.

4 Blue C Sushi
MAP D2 ■ 3411 Fremont Ave N
■ (206) 633-3411 ■ $$

A *kaiten*-style sushi restaurant, Blue C Sushi has a conveyor belt that delivers sushi and teriyaki dishes to diners. The seaweed salad is a surprise hit.

5 Paseo
MAP D2 ■ 4225 Fremont Ave N ■ (206) 545-7440 ■ No credit cards ■ $

This busy eatery churns out some of the most lauded sandwiches in Seattle. The most popular are Caribbean Roast and Paseo Press.

6 Hale's Ales Brewery
MAP C2 ■ 4301 Leary Way NW
■ (206) 706-1544 ■ $

Customers sip on the latest concoctions brewed in one of the city's first brewpubs *(see p53)*.

7 Qazis Indian Curry House
MAP D2 ■ 473 N 36th St
■ (206) 632-3575 ■ $$

One of the best purveyors of classic Indian cuisine, Qazis takes no short-cuts. Try the vegetable koftas, lamb korma, and *bharta* dishes.

8 Uneeda Burger
MAP D2 ■ 4302 Fremont Ave N
■ (206) 547-2600 ■ $$

A friendly eatery serving tasty burgers and sides. Also on offer are delicious milkshakes and a selection of beers.

9 El Camino
MAP D2 ■ 607 N 35th
■ (206) 632-7303 ■ $$

This is the place for great Mexican dishes using ingredients such as duck, pork, shrimp, fish, and chipotle peppers. Don't miss the margaritas.

10 Red Door
MAP D2 ■ 3401 Evanston Ave N ■ (206) 547-7521 ■ $$

Red Door draws huge crowds for its excellent microbrews and tastefully prepared pub food. The burgers, salads, and sandwiches are superb.

Bar at Red Door microbrewery

TOP10 Ballard

In the late 19th century, Scandinavian loggers and fishermen established a working waterfront, which is still functioning today. Seattle annexed Ballard in 1907, taking advantage of the huge economic growth the mill town fostered; by then Ballard was the state's third largest city. The late 1990s dot-com boom made real estate prices skyrocket, and led to the opening of new boutiques, art galleries, and restaurants. Popular tourist attractions include the Hiram M. Chittenden Locks and Golden Gardens. The Nordic Heritage Museum celebrates the culture of the area's Scandinavian Americans, and every May 17, the Norwegian Constitution Day Parade takes over the streets.

Moorings at Fishermen's Terminal

BALLARD

1 Top 10 Sights
see pp97–9

① Places to Eat
see p101

① Shops
see p100

0 meters 800
0 yards 800

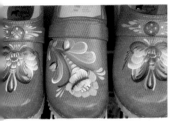

Clogs in the Nordic Heritage Museum

1 Nordic Heritage Museum

MAP B1 ■ 2655 NW Market St ■ Open 10am–4pm Tue–Sat & noon–4pm Sun ■ Adm ■ www.nordicmuseum.org

With rooms organized by country, this museum illustrates the links between the Scandinavian people in the Pacific Northwest. Founded in 1980, it is the only museum in the United States to revere the legacy of immigrants from the five Nordic countries – Finland, Iceland, Norway, Denmark, and Sweden. Visitors are enlightened by rotating and permanent exhibits, including colorful Old World textiles, rare china, books and bibles, woodworking tools, and carved wooden ale bowls. There is also an extensive music library.

2 Carl S. English Jr. Botanical Gardens

MAP B1 ■ 3015 NW 54th St ■ Open 9am–7pm daily

Take a little time for a delightful promenade through the greenery of lush trees and rare and exotic plants that fill the garden's 7 acres (3 ha), bordering the locks on the northern side of the Ship Canal. The gift shop, which also serves visitors to the locks, offers a guide to help visitors identify the plants.

Verdant borders, Botanical Gardens

3 Salmon Bay Industries

MAP B2

With the opening of the Sinclair Mill in the 1890s, Ballard was given the title "Shingle Capital of the World", as it was instrumental in rebuilding Seattle after the havoc wreaked by the Great Fire of 1889 (see p36). Smaller firms and manufacturers, machine shops, and foundries settled in to stake their claims as well. Today, the area has not changed much. Skirting Ballard's southern waterfront along the Ship Canal, Salmon Bay is home to many maritime and gravel-making industries.

Ballard Avenue and Market Street

NW 56TH ST

NW ⑩ MARKET ST

BERGEN PLACE

22TH AVE NORTHWEST

LEARY AVE NW

20TH AVE NW

TALLMAN AVE NW

NW CENTRAL PL

RUSSELL AVE NW

OLD BALLARD

④ ⑨ ①
③ ⑩
⑥ ⑨
⑩ ⑩
④ ⑦ ⑦

NW VERNON PL

LEARY AVE NW LONE PL

SHILSHOLE AVE NW

BURKE-GILMAN TRAIL EXTENSION

20TH AVE NW

BALLARD AVE NW

⑤

NW DOCK PL

⑤

⑧

Salmon Bay

Ballard Mill Marina

0 meters 150
0 yards 150

4 Ballard Locks

Every year, 100,000 vessels pass through the Ship Canal's Hiram M. Chittenden Locks (see pp26–7), and nearly as many tourists come to marvel at the site between Salmon Bay and Shilshole Bay. Named after a retired US Army Corps of Engineers general, the locks are the result of sophisticated engineering, and the sheer variety of pleasure boats and industrial ships that are able to pass through impress visitors. The locks also feature fish ladders to allow migrating salmon to leave from or return to their home streams, which is best observed between June and November. Do not miss the small but fascinating visitors' center, with its informative short film and displays.

A boat emerging from a lock

5 Golden Gardens
MAP P2

Ballard's largest park includes 87 acres (35 ha) of forested trails, beaches, picnic areas, and views of the Olympic Mountains and Puget Sound. Originally, the gardens stood at the end of the line for streetcars, which were funded by realtors who wanted Seattle residents to get away from the city. Cool summer nights bring groups to huddle around bonfires, while sunny days see hundreds getting tans or playing volleyball. There is also a dog area, and a boat ramp at the marina (see p47).

Golden Gardens waterfront

6 Fishermen's Terminal
MAP C2 ▪ 3919 18th Ave W

The terminal provides moorage for more than 700 commercial fishing vessels and workboats. Because of the sheltered port and the area's industries and businesses, many Northwest commercial fishermen regard Seattle as the best center for maintenance and repair. The bronze-and-stone Fishermen's Memorial sculpture, inscribed with the names of more than 500 local men and women, commemorates lives lost while fishing in Alaska. There are two seafood restaurants here – one is a take-out with dockside tables.

7 Ballard Avenue
MAP B1

From the roaring 1890s through the Great Depression, the four-block stretch of brick-paved Ballard Avenue defined the raison d'être of a mill town that also had a thriving boatbuilding and fishing industry. The 19th-century architecture is gorgeous, and it is easy to imagine a street filled with timber millworkers, salty fishermen, fishmongers, and the banks, saloons, and bordellos that served them. In 1976, Sweden's King Carl XVI Gustaf read the proclamation that listed Ballard Avenue on the Register of Historic Places.

8 Bardahl Sign
MAP C1

Whether traveling on foot or by bicycle, car, bus, boat, or plane, the towering, flashing, red neon advertisement for Bardahl automotive oil treatment is unmissable. From distant hilltops, the sign's manic ascending flashes harken back to the industrial roots of Ballard, and to company founder Ole Bardahl – Ballard resident and Norwegian immigrant. The sign is one of Seattle's favorite landmarks.

Sunday Farmers' Market entrance

⑨ Sunday Farmers' Market
MAP B2 ■ Open 10am–3pm

Like many neighborhoods in Seattle, Ballard attracts weekend shoppers by organizing for regional farmers, artists, and craftspeople to fill the closed-off streets around Ballard Avenue with an Old World market. The market operates year-round, but when summer is in full swing, growers from the arid east side of the Cascade Mountains bring their bounty of organic produce.

⑩ Market Street
MAP B1

The nerve center of Ballard has a vast selection of Scandinavian gift shops, stores, cafés, and taverns lining both sides of the street. The street's melange of local businesses and creative signage reflects the community's small-town personality that has remained intact since the days before Ballard officially became part of Seattle.

A MORNING WALK DOWN BALLARD AVENUE

▶ MORNING

Begin at the terminus of Ballard Avenue at **Market Street**. Walk down the west side of the street. Check out the gear at **Kavu** *(5419 Ballard Ave NW)*, an independent retailer of active wear that is appropriate for everything from walking in woodland to dining out. Cross the street to **Dandelion Botanical Company** *(see p100)* for natural apothecary items. Where 22nd Avenue meets Ballard Avenue, there is a large, brick **bell tower**, rebuilt from the original when Ballard's City Hall tower was destroyed by Seattle's devastating 1965 earthquake. Next, **Horseshoe** *(see p100)* entices with a luxurious boutique featuring local and European designer clothing and makeup. At the following intersection, notice the highly stylized roof crest of the **Ballard Inn** *(5300 Ballard Ave NW)*, which still has a "Bank Building" sign from its previous occupier over a century ago.

Cross the street and look out for the **Tractor Tavern** *(see p53)*, a musical outlet for local and touring musicians who play jazz and country rock. **Second Ascent** *(see p45)* specializes in clothing and gear for budget-minded fans of outdoor recreation. Find a remnant of days gone by at **Filson** *(5101 Ballard Ave NW)*, an outdoor clothing store founded in 1897, which opened a second location in 2016 in this 1904 building. After a long morning in the shops, turn back and stop in **The Other Coast Café** *(see p101)* for its selection of East-Coast-style sandwiches.

See map on pp96–7

Shops

Furnishings on sale, Camelion Design

1 Camelion Design
MAP C1 ■ 5330 Ballard Ave NW ■ (206) 783-7125 ■ www.camelion design.com

An eclectic array of home furnishings, from sofas to lamps and candles, awaits at this contemporary home decor store.

2 Scandinavian Specialties
MAP C1 ■ 6719 15th Ave NW ■ www.scanspecialties.com

The place for all things Scandinavian, with a focus on Norwegian goods. Groceries, sweets, books, household items, and souvenirs are found here.

3 Fair Trade Winds
MAP B1 ■ 5329 Ballard Ave NW ■ (206) 743-8500 ■ www.fairtrade winds.net

This store sells fair-trade crafts from all around the world. It is a great place to find unusual Christmas ornaments.

4 Horseshoe
MAP B1 ■ 5344 Ballard Ave NW ■ www.shophorseshoe.com

Award-winning women's boutique with a well-chosen collection featuring both local and international designers. The friendly staff add to the charm.

5 Card Kingdom
MAP C2 ■ 5105 Leary Ave NW ■ (206) 523-2273 ■ www.card kingdom.com

Play board games in the café, or choose from the large selection for sale, both classic and unusual.

6 Secret Garden Books
MAP B1 ■ 2214 NW Market St ■ (206) 789-5006 ■ www.secret gardenbooks.com

This small neighborhood bookstore, which opened in 1977, has a great selection of new and used books. It also hosts events and readings.

7 Prism
MAP B1 ■ 5208 Ballard Ave NW ■ (206) 402-4706 ■ www. prismseattle.com

People come here for a selection of ultrahip clothing, accessories, cool bags and backpacks, and design pieces.

8 Dandelion Botanical Company
MAP B2 ■ 5424 Ballard Ave NW ■ (206) 545-9842 ■ www. dandelionbotanical.com

Opened in 1996, this urban herbal apothecary stocks organic herbs, medicinal oils and tinctures, teas, and bath and body supplies.

9 Lucca Great Finds
MAP B2 ■ 5332 Ballard Ave NW ■ (206) 782-7337 ■ www.luccagreat finds.com

A rummage in this unique store turns up colorful candles, beautifully restored chandeliers, large old birdcages, antique cards, and maps.

10 re-soul
MAP C1 ■ 5319 Ballard Ave NW ■ (206) 789-7312 ■ www.resoul.com

This super stylish shoe store is known for its upscale European and American shoes. Also for sale are nifty bags, fashion accessories, and modern and retro home furnishings.

Places to Eat

PRICE CATEGORIES

Price categories include a three-course meal for one, two glasses of wine, and all unavoidable extra charges including tax.

$ under $40 $$ $40–80 $$$ over $80

1 Lockspot Café
MAP B1 ■ 3005 NW 54th ■ (206) 789-4865 ■ $

This eatery combines American staples at the busy takeout window, with a bar and a restaurant inside.

2 Hot Cakes
MAP B1 ■ 5427 Ballard Ave NW ■ (206) 453-3792 ■ $$

Dessert, Hot Cakes

Enjoy a delicious, gooey cake, with or without ice cream, or try one of the boozy milkshakes and ice cream floats at this popular spot.

3 La Carta de Oaxaca
MAP B1 ■ 5431 Ballard Ave NW ■ (206) 782-8722 ■ $

Make a beeline for this stylish Mexican eatery, and select from several entrees. The spartan decor is unusual – wall art consists of backlit photos of the region from where all the flavors originate.

4 Hattie's Hat
MAP B1 ■ 5231 Ballard Ave NW ■ (206) 784-0175 ■ $

A great place for huge breakfasts and classic American diner standards with a twist. Go for the Guinness stout meatloaf, homemade creamed corn, sweet potato fries, and braised southern greens.

5 Salmon Bay Café
MAP B2 ■ 5109 Shilshole Ave NW ■ (206) 782-5539 ■ Breakfast & lunch only ■ $

This bastion of inexpensive eats attracts blue-collar workers and a large youth crowd. The omelets are particularly popular.

6 The Other Coast Café
MAP B1 ■ 5315 Ballard Ave NW ■ (206) 789-0936 ■ $

Stick to basics such as the Reuben or the 12-inch meat or vegetarian subs at this New York-style deli.

7 India Bistro
MAP B1 ■ 2301 NW Market St ■ (206) 783-5080 ■ $

Recommended dishes here include spinach or mustard greens with paneer, spicy daal, and succulent lamb or chicken tandoori.

8 The Walrus and the Carpenter
MAP C2 ■ 4743 Ballard Ave NW ■ (206) 395-9227 ■ $$

A tiny place that serves mounds of oysters and fresh seafood (see p55).

9 Ray's Boathouse & Café
MAP A1 ■ 6049 Seaview Ave NW ■ (206) 789-3770 ■ $$ (café); $$$ (boathouse)

Classic seafood dishes and waterfront views make this a favorite (see p54).

Diners eating at Stoneburner

10 Stoneburner
MAP B2 ■ 5214 Ballard Ave NW ■ (206) 695-2051 ■ www.stoneburner seattle.com ■ $$$

A top restaurant for fresh seafood, wood-fired pizza, and a cocktail menu with non-alcoholic options.

See map on pp96–7

10 **West Seattle**

A stretch of Elliott Bay separates central Seattle from the peninsula of West Seattle, the city's oldest and largest district. Connected by a high freeway bridge and a lower span, West Seattle's proximity to both downtown and the Industrial District has always made it a popular residential area. It has attracted a population of younger, entrepreneurial residents drawn by lower housing costs and some of the best parklands in the city. Alki Beach brings hordes of people when the long, damp winter months give way to sunnier spring days.

Alki Point Lighthouse

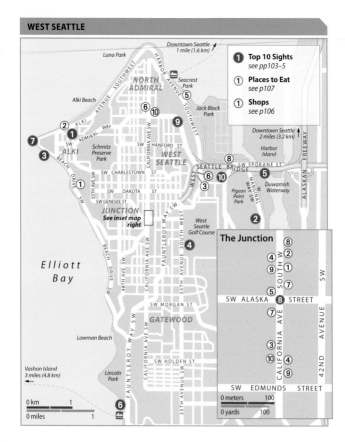

WEST SEATTLE

1 Log House Museum
MAP A5 ■ 3003 61st Ave SW ■ (206) 938-5293 ■ Open noon–4pm Thu–Sun ■ Suggested donation: $3 (adult), $1 (child); tours $2 ■ www.loghousemuseum.info

The museum, near Alki Beach, takes local history seriously – it marks the location where Captain Folger steered his schooner *Exact* in 1851, bringing to the region the families of Seattle's earliest pioneers, including the Arthur A. Denny party *(see p36)*. The museum explores the history of the Duwamish Peninsula with an orientation center, exhibits that preserve the community's legacy, speaker programs, and some special events.

2 Duwamish Longhouse and Cultural Center
MAP B6 ■ 4705 W Marginal Way SW ■ (206) 431-1582 ■ 10am–5pm Mon–Sat ■ www.duwamishtribe.org

This longhouse is a replica of the one which was used by the ancient Duwamish tribe for thousands of years before Seattle became a city. Cultural and educational events are held here and provide a fascinating insight into how the culture of the Native American tribe has survived and evolved.

3 Constellation Park
MAP A5

Seattle beachcombers check for the year's lowest tides and head to one of the best shoreline secrets, Constellation Park. It is not the best recreational shore, because it lacks a wide sandy stretch, but it gets its name from the large numbers of sea stars (starfish) clinging to the rocky intertidal zone. If the conditions are right, it is common to find scores of colorful sea stars, along with the usual anemones, gargantuan sea snails, and geoducks – Puget Sound's giant clams.

4 Camp Long
MAP B6 ■ 5200 35th SW ■ (206) 684-7434

Even though it is located in an entirely urban locale, Camp Long manages to come close to imparting the wild and natural experiences that are usually found only during hikes in the local mountain ranges. Once the 1941-era camp served only scouting organizations, but in 1984, the 68-acre (28-ha) compound opened to the general public. Inside the grounds, visitors can hike trails, learn about the environment from professional naturalists, or even rent rustic cabins for inner-city camping. One of the most popular attractions is the 20-ft- (6-m-) high Schurman climbing rock, carefully designed to incorporate every climbing maneuver. Bats, northern flying squirrels, opossums, racoons, and chipmunks have been sighted in the camp. Weekly interpretive walks, rock-climbing classes, and a golf course are also available.

Totem pole, Log House Museum

Cabin in the woods, Camp Long

5 West Seattle Bridge
MAP B5

From downtown, the fastest way to anywhere in West Seattle is via this highway crossing, built in 1984. The bridge takes traffic from the interstate I-5 and other feeder streets over the man-made Harbor Island and the mouth of the Duwamish River, and through to all the major streets in West Seattle. It is visible from many vantage points in town.

View from Fauntleroy Ferry Terminal

DREDGING THE DUWAMISH

Before white settlers landed in what would become Seattle, the Duwamish River zigzagged throughout the valley between the hillsides of West Seattle and Beacon Hill to the east. The area was in many ways more wetland than river until the Army Corps of Engineers dredged it in the late 19th century, deepening the bed and making the Duwamish permanently navigable by large commercial vessels. The dredge created Harbor Island, which lies between two small channels where the Duwamish pours into Elliott Bay.

6 Fauntleroy Ferry Terminal
MAP P3

The Fauntleroy Ferry is the only ferry from Seattle that travels to pastoral Vashon Island, and its terminal is located at the end of Fauntleroy Way. Unlike the downtown terminal, this one is located in a residential neighborhood, adjacent to scenic Lincoln Park (see p46). Allow some time to walk along the water's edge to watch ferries come and go. For a memorable visit to Vashon, bring a bike, and visit the pick-yourself berry patches in summer months.

7 Alki Point
MAP A5

The first Europeans to settle the region were Seattle pioneer Arthur A. Denny (see p36) and his party aboard the ship *Exact*; they chose the beachhead of West Seattle to come ashore in 1851. Duwamish Tribe Chief Sealth (see p37) met the group with open arms and began a long friendship with Seattle's founders. Today, Alki Point boasts rows of upscale waterfront condos for the well-to-do, and a great beach for shell hunting or scuba diving.

Waterfront path, Alki Beach

8 The Junction
MAP A6

The name refers to the intersection where California Avenue and Alaska Street meet, and it is here that the bulk of West Seattle's restaurants and shops are located. The small-town feel is palpable as you stroll along California Avenue past mom 'n' pop shops, and notice old-timers out for walks or sipping coffee at sidewalk tables. Murals painted on the sides of businesses mirror the warmth and pride of a tight-knit community in its prime, and reflect on its 150-year-old history.

Belvedere Park

9 Belvedere Park Viewpoint
MAP B5 ■ 3600 Admiral Way SW

For a bird's-eye view of the city of Seattle and the countryside beyond, simply drive or take a bus up Admiral Way to tiny Belvedere Park. Take in 180-degree picture-postcard views of the Cascade Range behind the high-rises of downtown, industrial Harbor Island, and the Port of Seattle's container yards, as well as Elliott Bay and Puget Sound. On clear days, the distant and permanently snow-capped Mount Baker on the north-eastern horizon looms above all else.

10 Steel Mill
MAP B5

Seattle's remaining steel mill sits on the Duwamish River's western shore. The mill processes recycled scrap from cans, cars, and construction materials just across the river from an upscale yacht marina and office park, embodying Seattle's ethic of a mixed-use waterfront.

A MORNING AT ALKI BEACH

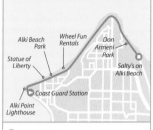

Alki Beach Park · Wheel Fun Rentals · Don Armeni Park · Statue of Liberty · Salty's on Alki Beach · Coast Guard Station · Alki Point Lighthouse

 MORNING

Experience the scenic Alki Avenue via a leisurely walk and easy bike ride along a waterfront trail (about 3.5 miles – 5.5 km – each way). Begin at the **Coast Guard Station** *(3201 Alki Ave)* which offers tours of the **Alki Point Lighthouse** on weekends from June to August (1:30–4:30pm). Walking northeast, stop at 63rd Ave SW to see the monument erected to celebrate the arrival of Seattle's early settlers. At 61st Ave SW, just before **Alki Beach Park** begins, look for the miniature **Statue of Liberty** on the right, built in 1952 on the strip of land dubbed "New York Alki" by the early settlers.

The sandy stretch of Alki Beach begins around 60th Ave. Stroll until 53rd Ave while taking in the views of Puget Sound, its ships and sailboats to the north, and the Olympic Mountains to the west. Rent a beach bike nearby at **Wheel Fun Rentals** *(see p111)* and continue along the trail. Public restrooms are available at the intersection of 57th Ave SW. As the road curves and becomes Harbor Ave, have a look through the telescopes set up above the seawall for more great views. Near the 1100 block of Harbor Ave look out for **Don Armeni Park**, where wedding parties and professional photographers often congregate to snap pictures of the city skyline. Stop at **Salty's on Alki Beach** *(see p107)* for a seriously scrumptious brunch that includes an all-you-can-eat Dungeness crab and other seafood indulgences.

See map on p102 ←

Shops

Numerous stylish objects for sale at Click! Design That Fits

① Click! Design that Fits
MAP B5 ▪ 4540 California Ave SW ▪ (206) 328-9252 ▪ www.click designthatfits.com

Meticulously designed paper crafts, books, kitchen goods, interior design items, and artwork are sold here.

② Carmilia's
MAP A6 ▪ 4528 California Ave SW ▪ (206) 935-1329 ▪ www.shop carmilias.com

Along with assorted accessories and jewelry for women, this boutique sells apparel by designers Nanette Lepore, Ella Moss, and Hanky Panky.

③ Northwest Art & Frame
MAP A6 ▪ 4733 California Ave SW ▪ (206) 937-5507

This welcoming store offers an enormous selection of custom and ready-made frames, art supplies, cards, stationery, and gift items.

④ Thunder Road Guitars
MAP B5 ▪ 4736 California Ave SW ▪ (206) 678-5248 ▪ www.thunder roadguitars.com

Beautifully restored electric and acoustic guitars are available here. Snap up the cables, and all the extras.

⑤ Easy Street Records
MAP A6 ▪ 4559 California Ave SW ▪ (206) 938-3279 ▪ www.easy streetonline.com

Shop here for the latest indie rock albums, then stop off for lunch and an espresso in the café.

⑥ Avalon Glassworks
MAP B5 ▪ 2914 SW Avalon Way ▪ (206) 937-6369

Watch artists create blown-glass vases, sculpture, ornaments, and seasonal items in myriad shapes, colors, and sizes in this exciting workshop.

⑦ Pharmaca Integrative Pharmacy
MAP A6 ▪ 4707 California Ave SW ▪ (206) 932-4225 ▪ www.pharmaca.com

The professional and personalized service focuses on wellness here.

⑧ West Seattle Computers
MAP A6 ▪ 2735 California Ave SW ▪ (206) 937-6800

The technical staff at this computer store are as friendly as they are tech savvy. Buy software or hardware, or have any digital problems solved.

⑨ Curious Kidstuff
MAP A6 ▪ 4740 California Ave SW ▪ (206) 937-8788 ▪ www. curiouskidstuff.com

Find all manner of treasures for children at this fun and welcoming toy store. There is a large selection of eco-friendly and wooden toys.

⑩ Metropolitan Market
MAP B5 ▪ 2320 42nd Ave SW ▪ (206) 937-0551 ▪ $

This neighborhood supermarket and gourmet purveyor of prepared food offers a selection of pasta dishes, paninis and customized salads. The store also sells quality kitchenware.

Places to Eat

PRICE CATEGORIES
Price categories include a three-course meal for one, two glasses of wine, and all unavoidable extra charges including tax.

$ under $40 $$ $40–80 $$$ over $80

1 La Rustica
MAP A5 ▪ 4100 Beach Drive SW ▪ (206) 932-3020 ▪ $$

Dine on exquisite Italian classics, such as spaghetti with garlic prawns, or pizza with mushrooms and prosciutto ham.

2 Phoenecia
MAP A5 ▪ 2716 Alki Ave SW ▪ (206) 935-6550 ▪ $

Visit Phoenecia to enjoy delicious tapas, gourmet pizzas, or wonderful lamb dishes. During the summer months customers can dine outside, with lovely views of the beach.

3 Luna Park Café
MAP B5 ▪ 2918 SW Avalon Way ▪ (206) 935-7250 ▪ $

Inside this café, the kitschy artifacts and decor reflect the style of the 1950s. Popular basics feature on the menu, including the BLT and club sandwiches, hand-dipped malted milkshakes, and classic cobb salad.

4 Azuma Sushi
MAP A6 ▪ 4533 California Ave SW ▪ (206) 937-1148 ▪ $

Insiders return here often for their fix of professionally prepared sushi and sashimi, sake, and teriyaki at very reasonable prices.

5 Salty's on Alki Beach
MAP B5 ▪ 1936 Harbor Ave SW ▪ (206) 937-1600 ▪ $$

The specials board at Salty's reflects the freshest seasonal fish and seafood available, and picture windows offer diners the most breathtaking views across Elliott Bay.

6 Mission Cantina
MAP A5 ▪ 2325 California Ave SW ▪ (206) 937-8220 ▪ $

Head to Mission for Latin American food and great margaritas.

7 Jak's Grill
MAP A6 ▪ 4548 California Ave SW ▪ (206) 937-7809 ▪ $

This steakhouse prepares superb beef, chicken, and seafood dishes, and the price also includes several side orders.

Burger, Chelan Café

8 Chelan Café
MAP B5 ▪ 3527 Chelan Ave SW ▪ (206) 932-7383 ▪ $

Dine on typical, good-value American truck-stop fare here, including burgers, fries, meatloaf, and eggs.

9 West 5
MAP A6 ▪ 4539 California Ave SW ▪ (206) 937-1966 ▪ $

Munch on comfort food such as BLTs and burgers at this hip eatery.

Desserts at Bakery Nouveau

10 Bakery Nouveau
MAP A6 ▪ 4737 California Ave SW ▪ (206) 923-0534 ▪ $

This award-winning bakery always has lines for its inviting assortment of fresh, buttery, flaky treats. The friendly staff also serve gourmet coffee drinks and delicious pizzas.

See map on p102

Streetsmart

Neon food stall signs along
Seattle's Pike Place Market

Getting To and Around Seattle

Arriving by Air

Sea-Tac International Airport (SEA) lies about 10 miles (16 km) south of Seattle and is served by dozens of carriers, including **British Airways**, **Delta**, and **Lufthansa**, along with budget airlines, such as **Southwest Air**. There are non-stop flights from London, Frankfurt, Paris, Amsterdam, and a few other European hubs, and non-stop flights to Hong Kong, Shanghai, Beijing, Seoul, and Tokyo. The easiest way to get into Seattle is via light rail – look for the signs.

Arriving by Seaplane

Kenmore Air has a fleet of seaplanes offering tours of Puget Sound, the Olympic Mountains to the west, and the Cascades to the east. Kenmore also serves several destinations in British Columbia, Canada. Flights land on the water in Lake Union, just north of downtown.

Traveling by Bus

Bolt Bus runs express services from Seattle to Portland or Vancouver, Canada. **Greyhound** also has an extensive network of buses; they stop more frequently so travel times can be longer.

Traveling by Rail

Seattle's King Street Station is the depot for **Amtrak** passenger trains from Vancouver, British Columbia, and all points south and east. The Coast Starlight travels between Los Angeles and Seattle, and the Amtrak Cascades itineraries serve stops between Eugene, Oregon, and Vancouver. Although the Cascades line is reliable, the Coast Starlight regularly experiences delays; it is not the best choice for those needing to make a connection in another destination. Be aware that Amtrak runs buses rather than trains on some of its routes.

Traveling by Commuter Rail

Seattle's commuter rail service, **Sound Transit**, links King Street Station with Everett, Edmonds, Kent, Sumner, Auburn, Tukwila, Puyallup, and Tacoma. Service is limited, though; check online for the relevant time schedule.

Traveling by Ferry

For a fantastic way to experience Seattle and its environs, consider taking a ferry. Major routes operated by **Washington State Ferries** include: Seattle-Bremerton and Seattle-Winslow (on Bainbridge Island) from Pier 52, and West Seattle-Vashon Island and West Seattle-Southworth from the Fauntleroy terminal. There is a shuttle that takes ferry passengers from the ferry dock in West Seattle to the Alki Beach business district and the Alaska Junction business district, which is free with a ferry ticket. From Anacortes, some distance north of Seattle, there is a ferry service to the San Juan Islands and Sydney (on Vancouver Island, north of Victoria).

Traveling by Public Transit

King County Metro Transit offers the most affordable transportation option. Pay on entry for buses heading downtown, and on leaving for buses heading away from downtown. If connecting with another bus, ask for a free transfer from the driver. Most buses are equipped with wheelchair lifts. King County Metro Transit includes the light rail, with its service to Sea-Tac, and the South Lake Union Trolley.

Be sure to buy an ORCA pass – a regional transit card – from the Westlake Tunnel transit station or the metro customer service office downtown, open 8:30am to 4:30pm, Monday to Friday. Tickets and cards for buses are available from machines at most light rail stations.

Traveling by Car and by Taxi

A car can be handy, but in the heart of downtown Seattle it may be more trouble than it is worth. Traffic is usually heavy and parking expensive – a **Seattle Yellow Cab** is often a better option. App-based car-sharing services, such as **Uber** and **Lyft**, are common. It costs about $45 for a taxi from the airport to the downtown hotel district. There are plenty of rental car counters at the airport, but most rental lots are located offsite and are reachable by shuttle from the arrivals level. There are several rental car lots downtown for those who do not need a car for their entire trip – also avoiding the airport surcharge. If reserving a car ahead, make sure to select a downtown pickup location. Popular rental firms include **Enterprise Rent-A-Car**, **Avis**, and **National Car Rental**. Insurance is required, which can be purchased from the rental company for those who do not already have cover.

Traveling by Bicycle

Seattle's hilly landscape means biking is not necessarily the best option, but there are a few easy trails along Alki Beach in West Seattle (see p104), and more adventurous cyclists can ride the Burke-Gilman Trail (see p93) to Redmond, 16 miles (25 km) east of the city.

Cyclists are much safer on paths reserved for non-motorized vehicles. There is a city-wide law that requires riders to wear helmets. A good rental company is **Wheel Fun Rentals**. Some hotels have free loaner bicycles, so ask at the front desk.

Getting Around on Foot

As with cycling, Seattle's hills and stair climbs can be daunting, but walking is a great way to explore the city. Walking tours led by **Seattle Architecture Foundation** explore the University of Washington campus, Pike Place Market, the architecture and history of Pioneer Square, and there are a wide range of food tours, including through the International District. The city council offers a downloadable **Seattle Recreational Walking Map** on its website, which outlines popular routes.

DIRECTORY

ARRIVING BY AIR

British Airways
w britishairways.com

Delta
w delta.com

Lufthansa
w lufthansa.com

Sea-Tac International Airport (SEA)
17801 International Blvd
((206) 787-5388
w portseattle.org/
Sea-Tac

Southwest Air
w southwest.com

ARRIVING BY SEAPLANE

Kenmore Air
((866) 435-9524
w kenmoreair.com

TRAVELING BY BUS

Bolt Bus
((877) 265-8287
w boltbus.com

Greyhound
503 S Royal Brougham Way
((206) 624-0618
w greyhound.com

TRAVELING BY RAIL

Amtrak
MAP K6 ■ 303 S Jackson St
((800) 872-7245
w amtrak.com

TRAVELING BY COMMUTER RAIL

Sound Transit
((888) 889-6368
w soundtransit.org

TRAVELING BY FERRY

Washington State Ferries
((206) 464-6400
w wsdot.wa.gov/ferries

TRAVELING BY PUBLIC TRANSIT

King County Metro Transit
((206) 553-3000
w kingcounty.gov/
depts/transportation/
metro.aspx

TRAVELING BY CAR AND BY TAXI

Avis
((206) 223-3499
w avis.com

Enterprise Rent-A-Car
((206) 382-1051
w enterprise.com

Lyft
w lyft.com

National Car Rental
MAP K4 ■ 1601 3rd Ave
((888) 445-5664
w nationalcar.com

Seattle Yellow Cab
w seattleyellowcab.com

Uber
w uber.com

TRAVELING BY BICYCLE

Wheel Fun Rentals
MAP A5 ■ 2530 Alki Ave
((206) 932-2035
w wheelfunrentals.com

GETTING AROUND ON FOOT

Seattle Architecture Foundation
((888) 377-4510
w seattlearchitecture.org

Seattle Recreational Walking Map
w seattle.gov/
transportation/
walk_map.htm

Practical Information

Passports and Visas

Canadian citizens need proof of nationality to clear United States customs. Visitors from New Zealand, Australia, Japan, and most European countries must apply well in advance (and pay a fee) for entry clearance via the **Electronic System for Travel Authorization (ESTA)**. Other nationalities must have a passport that is valid for at least six months from the date of entry, and a visa obtained from a US consulate or embassy in their own country prior to traveling.

While in the US, visitors can contact their embassy for consular assistance. The **UK**, **New Zealand**, and **Ireland** do not have consulates in Seattle itself; nationals from these countries will need to call San Francisco or Los Angeles. **Australia's** consulate is not far from Sea-Tac Airport (see p110).

Customs Regulations

Federal law allows each visitor to bring in $100 worth of gifts, 1 liter of liquor, and 200 cigarettes, duty-free. Cash or negotiable funds exceeding $10,000 must be declared.

Travel Safety Advice

Visitors can get up-to-date travel safety information from the **UK Foreign and Commonwealth Office**, the **US Department of State**, and the **Australian Department of Foreign Affairs and Trade**.

Travel Insurance

It is wise, if not essential, to take out some travel insurance before traveling. Most policies will cover canceled flights and lost baggage in addition to medical expenses. Those with health insurance at home should save receipts from any incurred medical expenses during the trip.

Health

In an emergency, dial 911 to be connected to a dispatcher who will direct the call to the fire, police, or ambulance services.

All city hospitals have walk-in ERs (emergency rooms). Recommended hospitals include the **Virginia Mason Hospital** and **Harborview Hospital**. For less critical issues – minor injuries, illness, or sexual health issues – look for urgent care clinics inside **Bartell's** or **Walgreen's** convenience stores. A visit will cost around $150 and does not include medication costs.

Many big supermarkets have pharmacies on site, as do **Rite-Aid**, and the Walgreen's and Bartell's convenience stores. The pharmacist can usually advise on simple health problems. You should not have trouble finding the medication you need, but bring a doctor's letter and a copy of any prescription to avoid problems with customs officials or the pharmacist. Note the generic name, as well as the brand name, of any medication required. Drugs can be expensive in the US, so it is wise to prepare in advance by bringing extra medication from home.

Personal Security

Most tourists never venture near the edgier neighborhoods where economic disenfranchisement has helped foster street crime. Seattle's major streets and arterials are quite safe for sightseeing during the day. Feel free to stroll at night, though only if you already know the area comfortably.

Currency and Banking

The US currency is the dollar, and one dollar is made up of 100 cents. The counterfeit-proof bills can be difficult to distinguish from each other.

Look out for currency exchange offices in the main terminal and South Satellite at Sea-Tac Airport, as well as at major banks downtown.

Avoid bad rates by withdrawing cash from ATMs around town, where daily rates are more advantageous. There may be a small fee to use the ATM for those who are not customers of the bank (their own bank may charge, too). Check with the bank for charge rates before traveling.

Telephone and Internet

Seattle's area code is 206, but the vastness of surrounding suburbs has necessitated several pre-fixes. The Eastside (see pp62–3) is mostly covered by 425, while 253 covers south of the city, and 360 handles outlying areas. To call outside the 206 area code, dial 1, the area code, and the seven-digit number. Toll-free phone numbers begin with 800, 877, or 888. Dial 411 for directory assistance, 011 for an international call.

There is no shortage of coffee shops, cafés, and internet cafés in Seattle, most of which offer free and high-speed Wi-Fi services for any device. Seattle public libraries offer free internet access, though time limits will sometimes apply.

Postal Services

The **Main Post Office** is located at Third and Union in downtown Seattle. Almost all post offices have automated mailing stations where customers can weigh their items and buy postage without standing in line. Some drug stores, convenience stores, and supermarkets will also sell stamps, but they may not have proper international postage. Postcards cost $1.15 to send abroad.

TV, Radio, and Newspapers

Seattle has one major daily newspaper, covering current events and vital information, the *Seattle Times*. The Thursday and Friday editions include additional entertainment sections – useful for seeing what is happening around town. The *Seattle Post-Intelligencer* offers similar information, but is available online only. There are two public radio stations based in Seattle, **KUOW** (94.9 FM) and **KEXP** (90.3 FM), which broadcast programs based on news, current affairs, and pop music.

Opening Hours

Department stores and supermarkets are open seven days a week, and some of the larger ones stay open as late as 10pm on some nights. Banks are usually open 8am to 5pm Monday to Friday, but ATMs are plentiful and accessible at all times. Post offices are generally open 9am to 5pm Monday to Friday. Museums are open 10am–5pm, but they often stay open until 9pm one night a week. Bars will serve liquor until 2am.

DIRECTORY

PASSPORTS AND VISAS

Australian Consulate
MAP P5 ■ 401 Andover Park E
((206) 575-7446
w usa.embassy.gov.au

Electronic System for Travel Authorization (ESTA)
w esta.cbp.dhs.gov

Irish Consulate
((415) 392-4214
w dfa.ie/irish-consulate/sanfrancisco

New Zealand Consulate
((310) 566-6555
w safetravel.govt.nz/our-services

UK Consulate
((415) 617-1300
w gov.uk/government/world/organisations/british-consulate-general-san-francisco

TRAVEL SAFETY ADVICE

Australian Department of Foreign Affairs and Trade
w dfat.gov.au
w smartraveller.gov.au

UK Foreign and Commonwealth Office
w gov.uk/foreign-travel-advice

US Department of State
w travel.state.gov

HEALTH

Bartell's
MAP K4 ■ 1628 5th Ave
((206) 622-0581

Harborview Hospital
MAP L5 ■ 111 Jefferson St
((206) 744-5000

Rite-Aid
MAP K5 ■ 802 3rd Ave
((206) 623-0577

Virginia Mason Hospital
MAP L4 ■ 1010 Spring St
((206) 583-6433

Walgreen's
MAP J4 ■ 222 Pike St
((888) 227-3312

POSTAL SERVICES

Main Post Office
MAP K4 ■ 301 Union St

TV, RADIO, AND NEWSPAPERS

KEXP
w kexp.org

KUOW
w kuow.org

Seattle Post-Intelligencer
w seattlepi.com

Seattle Times
w seattletimes.com

Time Difference

Seattle keeps Pacific Standard Time (PST), eight hours behind GMT and three hours behind Eastern Standard Time (EST). Daylight saving time is observed between March and November.

Electrical Appliances

American current puts out 110 volts compared to Europe's 220. Almost all new appliances run dual voltage, but the outlets are a different shape so an adapter will be needed. Check device manuals to be sure. Most hotels, vacation rentals, and B&Bs supply hair dryers.

Weather

July is historically the driest month of the year, and late spring, summer, and early fall are the most mild and appealing times to visit. Most festivals and street fairs occur during the summer. Be prepared for rain all year round.

Travelers with Specific Needs

Disabled drivers may park in specially designated spaces if they have the proper vehicle identification from the **Department of Licensing**. Any unauthorized use may incur a $250 penalty.

Seattle's **King County Metro Transit** (see p111) and many other attractions offer discounted fares for senior citizens and the disabled. The Regional Reduced Fare Permit costs $3 and entitles you to reduced fares

on Community Transit, Metro Transit, Washington State Ferries, and Sound Transit. Visitors wishing to obtain such a pass will require an **American Disabilities Act (ADA) Paratransit Card**. National parks also issue special vehicle passes for the disabled that entitle all passengers in the vehicle to enter the park for free.

Seattle's metro system pioneered the use of Lift-U lifts on buses to accommodate those who use wheelchairs or have difficulty using stairs. Look for a wheelchair symbol posted next to the scheduled arrival times on placards at bus stops.

Any new construction in Seattle must conform to the ADA by providing easy access for those in wheelchairs. While newer restaurants and hotels will have met these requirements, it is best to call older establishments to check accessibility.

Every downtown corner provides ramped curbs, while most government buildings, supermarkets, tourist attractions, performance venues, and hotels have hands-free doorways and access ramps.

There is good disabled access to toilets in public restrooms, but these are rare in Seattle. There are public washrooms at the Pike Place Market.

Founded in 1965, **Sight Connection Community Services for the Blind and Partially Sighted** is a great resource for sight-impaired individuals. Seattle's Central Library offers a **Washington Talking Book & Braille Library** and an equal access library program.

Visitor Information

Visit Seattle provides information for a visit to Seattle, and **Washington State Tourism** is helpful for information on the rest of the state.

The Stranger and the *Seattle Weekly* both have excellent information online about events and activities. These free local papers can be found in cafés and corner newsboxes. The **Seattle Eater** is an up-to-date online source for the Seattle restaurant and bar scene.

Trips and Tours

There are many options for touring Seattle and the region. Walking tours explore Pike Place Market and the International District (see p111), **Seattle by Segway** run tours along the beach at Alki, **Argosy Cruises** take visitors through the Ballard Locks, and **Alki Kayak Tours** venture out to see the orcas that live in Puget Sound. Tour operators will also take tourists to harder-to-reach places, such as Mount Rainier and the Boeing Aircraft Factory.

Shopping

While there are a few department stores downtown, the best offering is at the shopping mall in either Bellevue or Tukwila, near the airport.

For unconventional shopping, Pike Place Market is a fine place for souvenirs; the north end of the market offers a full range of arts and crafts. The neighborhoods host weekly farmers' markets, selling preserves or vacuum-packed smoked salmon – a popular gift for those back home. Summer is craft fair time at the markets, when an overwhelming array of garden art, photography, and toys are sold.

Some stores will waive the sales tax for those who are not Washington residents – ask before you complete the transaction.

Dining

Seattle has an excellent farm-to-table and local food scene. Local chefs like Tamara Murphy, Tom Douglas, Ethan Stoll, and Thierry Rautureau make the most of the region's seasonal offerings – check the restaurant listings for Capitol Hill (see pp84–5) and downtown (see p77) for options.

Cheap eats are widely available. Look anywhere in the city's International District for dinners under $10. "The Ave" in the University District has great bargains too, thanks to the student population.

Accommodation

Major hotel chains – and a few boutique offerings – are located primarily downtown and around the Seattle Center. Capitol Hill has the highest concentration of B&Bs and smaller inns, with many set in beautifully renovated classic homes. East Capitol Hill can be quieter than downtown, while still being convenient to transit, and often, parking is included.

Vacation rentals are available all over the city, from single rooms in private homes to entire apartments. The cheapest stays will generally be at hostels. There are four in Seattle; offerings run from private rooms to shared bunks with a communal bathroom down the hall.

Seattle's occupancy rates are usually high, making last-minute bargains rare – therefore it is best to make reservations in advance, especially during summer and fall. Rooms under $150 per night are considered a good deal in Seattle – while standard and boutique hotels can start as high as $400 per night. Studio apartments via **Airbnb** start at around $70 per night, and basic hostel bunks are about $30 per night.

For those wishing to compare hotels and prices, there are many online booking services that offer substantial discounts on standard prices. Some recommended sites include **Expedia** and **Booking.com**.

DIRECTORY

TRAVELERS WITH SPECIFIC NEEDS

American Disabilities Act (ADA) Paratransit Cards
📞 (800) 514-0301
🌐 metro.kingcounty.gov/tops/accessible/programs/paratransit.html

Department of Licensing
📞 (306) 902-3900
🌐 dol.wa.gov/vehicle registration/parking.html

Sight Connection Community Services for the Blind and Partially Sighted
📞 (800) 458-4888
🌐 sightconnection.org

Washington Talking Book & Braille Library
📞 (800) 542-0866
🌐 wtbbl.org

VISITOR INFORMATION

Seattle Eater
🌐 eater.com

Seattle Weekly
🌐 seattleweekly.com

The Stranger
🌐 thestranger.com

Visit Seattle
MAP K4 ▪ 701 Pike St
📞 (206) 461-5800
🌐 visitseattle.org

Washington State Tourism
📞 (800) 544-1800
🌐 experiencewa.com

TRIPS AND TOURS

Alki Kayak Tours
MAP B5 ▪ 1660 Harbor Ave SW
📞 (206) 953-0237
🌐 kayakalki.com

Argosy Cruises
MAP J5 ▪ 1101 Alaskan Way, Pier 55
📞 (206) 623-1445
🌐 argosycruises.com

Seattle by Segway
📞 (206) 388-5508
🌐 seattlebysegway.com

ACCOMMODATION

Airbnb
🌐 airbnb.com

Booking.com
🌐 booking.com

Expedia
🌐 expedia.com

Places to Stay

PRICE CATEGORIES
For a standard, double room per night (with breakfast if included), taxes, and extra charges.

$ under $200 $$ $200–300 $$$ over $300

Downtown Hotels

Best Western Plus Pioneer Square

MAP K5 ▪ 77 Yesler Way ▪ 1-800-800-5514 ▪ www. pioneersquare.com ▪ $
History buffs and sports fans flock to this 19th-century landmark hotel featuring period decor and deluxe bathrooms. The bustling waterfront, ferry terminal, stadiums, and historic Pioneer Square are all nearby.

Courtyard Seattle Downtown/Lake Union

MAP J1 ▪ 925 Westlake Ave N ▪ (206) 213-0100 ▪ www.marriott.com ▪ $
One of Marriott's less expensive offerings, this hotel has great lake views and is close to Seattle Center and I-5. Rooms have free internet, and there is an indoor pool and fitness center. It is walking distance from the streetcar to downtown.

Hilton Seattle

MAP K4 ▪ 1301 6th Ave ▪ 1-800-426-0535 ▪ www. thehiltonseattle.com ▪ $
Set near the Convention Center, the Hilton is very popular with business travelers. All rooms are above the 14th floor, with fantastic views, and there is free web TV. Check out the senior citizen and family discount plans. There is also a rental car company located on-site.

Hotel Max

MAP K3 ▪ 620 Stewart St ▪ (206) 728-6299 ▪ www. hotelmaxseattle.com ▪ $
This hip boutique hotel is decorated with original art-work by local artists. Head to the lobby for locally roasted coffee in the morning or a selection of microbrews at happy hour.

Hotel Theodore

MAP K4 ▪ 1531 7th Ave ▪ 1-800-663-1144 ▪ www. hoteltheodore.com ▪ $
Located near downtown's best shopping, this hotel is named after the 26th president of the United States. Evenings bring live jazz piano to the lobby, where visitors gather to relax.

The Edgewater Hotel

MAP H4 ▪ 2411 Alaskan Way, Pier 67 ▪ 1-800-624-0670 ▪ www.edgewater hotel.com ▪ $$
All rooms combine luxury with Pacific Northwest charm. Features include handcrafted pine furni-ture, river rock fireplaces, Ralph Lauren bedding, deluxe bathroom amen-ities, and an in-room Starbucks coffee service.

Fairmont Olympic Hotel

MAP K4 ▪ 411 University St ▪ 1-888-363-5022 ▪ www.fairmont.com ▪ $$
One of Pacific Northwest's most lauded properties, this landmark hotel has treated guests with the utmost elegance and personalized service since it opened in 1924.

Grand Hyatt Seattle

MAP K3 ▪ 721 Pine St ▪ (206) 774-1234 ▪ www. grandseattle.hyatt.com ▪ $$
The deluxe rooms include free use of the sprawling health club, which has an exercise room, a sauna, a Jacuzzi, a steam bath, and cardio machines with flat-screen televisions.

Hotel Ändra

MAP J3 ▪ 2000 4th Ave ▪ (206) 448-8600 ▪ www. hotelandra.com ▪ $$
This sophisticated hotel offers top-notch service and a boutique experience to its guests. Scandinavian design elements can be seen in all of the 119 rooms and luxury suites.

Inn at the Market

MAP J4 ▪ 86 Pine St ▪ 1-800-446-4484 ▪ www. innatthemarket.com ▪ $$
This inn pampers guests in an enviable locale with panoramic mountain views. Dine at Campagne, the classic French restau-rant, or in its more casual country-style café.

Kimpton Hotel Vintage Seattle

MAP K4 ▪ 1100 5th Ave ▪ 1-800-853-3914 ▪ www. hotelvintage-seattle.com ▪ $$
Comforts at this upscale hotel include plush terry-cloth robes, lush fabrics, and cherry wood furni-ture. There is also a hosted wine hour by a wood-burning fireplace in

the lobby. Try Tulio, the award-winning Italian restaurant for a sumptuous dinner.

Loews Hotel 1000
MAP K4 ▪ 1000 1st Ave ▪ (206) 957-1000 ▪ www. loewshotel.com ▪ $$
An upscale hotel set in a great downtown location. Rooms feature fine Thai linens, two-person tubs, and state-of-the-art entertainment centers.

Mayflower Park Hotel
MAP J4 ▪ 405 Olive Way ▪ 1-800-426-5100 ▪ www. mayflowerpark.com ▪ $$
The Mayflower was built in 1927. Rooms reflect common 1920s Queen Anne design touches in subtle and dark hues. The house restaurant is Andaluca, a small, top-rated establishment with excellent Mediterranean fare. The adjoining bar, Oliver's, serves exquisite martinis.

Renaissance Seattle
MAP K5 ▪ 515 Madison St ▪ (206) 583-0300 ▪ www. marriott.com ▪ $$
This deluxe pet-friendly hotel has a penthouse swimming pool, a whirlpool tub, and a well-equipped workout room. It is located near many major tourist attractions.

Seattle Marriott Waterfront
MAP H4 ▪ 2100 Alaskan Way ▪ (206) 443-5000 ▪ www.marriott.com ▪ $$
This is Seattle's first full-service hotel with excellent views of Puget Sound and the Olympic Mountains. There is a fitness center and a great restaurant serving craft beer and artisanal wines.

W Seattle
MAP K4 ▪ 1112 4th Ave ▪ (206) 264-6000 ▪ www. wseattle.com ▪ $$
The sleek W attracts hip, trendy, and well-heeled folk. It offers modern amenities, impeccable hospitality (including the W's signature "Whatever/ Whenever" concierge service), and divinely comfortable beds.

The Westin Seattle
MAP K3 ▪ 1900 5th Ave ▪ (206) 728-1000 ▪ www. westinseattle.com ▪ $$
Located in two towers, the Westin has an indoor pool, fitness suite, 24-hour room service, a restaurant and lobby bar, valet/laundry, and a business center.

Alexis Hotel
MAP K5 ▪ 1007 1st Ave ▪ 1-866-356-8894 ▪ www. alexishotel.com ▪ $$$
Since 1901, the Alexis has lived up to its reputation as an elegant haven for those who like being pampered. Evening wine tasting, 24-hour room service, a steam and fitness room, a full-day spa, and the Bookstore Bar are highlights.

Neighborhood Hotels

Ace Hotel
MAP H3 ▪ 2423 1st Ave ▪ (206) 448-4721 ▪ www. acehotel.com ▪ $
This hotel, located in a historic building in the heart of Belltown, appeals to guests who prefer location over luxury. There are few amenities; instead the emphasis is on the ultra-modern decor. Both Pike Place Market and Capitol Hill are nearby.

Graduate Seattle
MAP E2 ▪ 4507 Brooklyn Ave NE ▪ 1-800-899-0251 ▪ www.graduatehotels. com ▪ $
An attractive choice for visiting parents, students, and professors, this award-winning hotel has designer rooms that offer comfortable beds and views of the U-District, the Space Needle, and the downtown skyline.

Inn at Queen Anne
MAP G2 ▪ 505 1st Ave N ▪ 1-800-952-5043 ▪ www. innatqueenanne.com ▪ $
There is a charm and a cozy ambience that characterizes this 1930s-era inn. Rooms have kitchenettes and there is a plant-filled patio/court-yard, which is a perfect place to sip tea or coffee.

MarQueen Hotel
MAP G1 ▪ 600 Queen Anne Ave N ▪ (206) 282-7407 ▪ www.marqueen. com ▪ $
Located in lively Lower Queen Anne, this stately hotel provides a wonderful alternative to the area's chain motels and hotels. It is a short walk to the quaint cafés, trendy bars, and small shops nearby.

University Inn
MAP E2 ▪ 4140 Roosevelt Way NE ▪ (206) 632-5055 ▪ www.universityinn seattle.com ▪ $
Parents and students reserve early to stay at the University Inn, only three blocks from the University of Washington. Guests help themselves to a free continental breakfast and a courtesy shuttle to downtown.

Watertown

MAP E2 ■ 4242 Roosevelt Way NE ■ (206) 826-4242 ■ www.watertownseattle.com ■ $

A hotel primarily catering for students and their parents, Watertown boasts non-smoking premises, free parking, loaner bicycles, and a free shuttle service to select attractions.

Sorrento Hotel

MAP L4 ■ 900 Madison St ■ 1-800-426-1265 ■ www.hotelsorrento.com ■ $$

At the opulent Sorrento, guests find Seattle's finest boutique hotel as well as a destination gourmet restaurant, the Hunt Club. Enjoy the Italian marble bathrooms, luxury linens, and a complimentary car service within downtown.

B&Bs and Guesthouses

11th Avenue Inn

MAP M3 ■ 121 11th Ave E ■ 1-800-720-7161 ■ No air conditioning ■ www.11thavenueinn.com ■ $

This quiet neighborhood B&B is housed in a lovely 1906 Victorian inn. The eight guestrooms are decorated with antique furnishings and boast modern amenities. All have queen beds and bathrooms. There is free parking and it is very close to downtown.

Bacon Mansion Bed & Breakfast

MAP E4 ■ 959 Broadway E ■ 1-800-240-1864 ■ No air conditioning ■ www.baconmansion.com ■ $

This 1909 Edwardian Tudor mansion exudes elegance with its original carved wood trim, 3,000- crystal chandelier, marble fireplaces, and remarkable library.

Bed & Breakfast on Broadway

MAP L1 ■ 722 Broadway E ■ (206) 329-8933 ■ No air conditioning ■ www.bbonbroadway.com ■ $

Located in a historical residential neighborhood north of Capitol Hill, the features here include a parlor with a grand piano, a fireplace, Oriental rugs, antiques, and polished hardwood floors.

Gaslight Inn

MAP E4 ■ 1727 15th Ave ■ (206) 325-3654 ■ No air conditioning ■ www.gaslight-inn.com ■ $

This lovingly restored 19th-century inn inspires guests with its private art collection. Highlights include a heated outdoor pool, fireplaces, and stunning views. Some rooms have a shared bathroom.

Mildred's B&B

MAP E4 ■ 1202 15th Ave E ■ 1-800-327-9692 ■ No air conditioning ■ www.mildredsbnb.com ■ $

This large, turreted 1890 Victorian inn takes guests back in time with lace curtains, red carpets, and a wrap-around front porch perfect for lounging.

Pensione Nichols

MAP J4 ■ 1923 1st Ave ■ (206) 441-7125 ■ No air conditioning ■ www.pensionenichols.com ■ $

Personalized services and its proximity to downtown make this B&B a decent in-city choice. It may be a little worn on the edges, but the views of sparkling Puget Sound are great.

Shafer Baillie Mansion

MAP E4 ■ 907 14th Ave E ■ (206) 322-4654 ■ www.sbmansion.com ■ $

This Tudor Revival building has clean, well-appointed rooms with private bathrooms and a beautiful wood-panelled dining room It is located within walking distance of the Seattle Asian Art Museum and Volunteer Park.

Greenlake Guest House

MAP D1 ■ 7630 E Greenlake N ■ (206) 729-8700 ■ www.greenlakeguesthouse.com ■ $$

Across the street from beautiful Green Lake, and close to restaurants and shops, this guesthouse has modern rooms with TVs and private bathrooms. Most rooms also have gas fireplaces.

Apartments and Private Homes

Belltown Inn

MAP J3 ■ 2301 3rd Ave ■ (206) 529-3700 ■ www.belltown-inn.com ■ $

Located in the heart of hip Belltown, this complex features fully furnished studios with kitchenettes. Bikes are available free of charge, or it is a short walk from Pike Place Market and is on the free Metro bus line.

First Hill Apartments

MAP M5 ■ 400 10th Ave ■ (206) 621-9229 ■ www.firsthillapts.com ■ $

A good, affordable choice close to downtown, this secure complex of apartments offers everything from tiny studios to luxury loft suites, all fully furnished and well equipped.

The Mediterranean Inn

MAP G1 ■ 425 Queen Anne Ave N ■ (866) 525-4700 ■ www. mediterranean-inn.com ■ $

Non-smoking, furnished studio apartments are offered here near Seattle Center. Each unit has a kitchenette. Parking is available for a fee, and there is a gym. It is in walking distance of downtown.

Seattle Suites

MAP K4 ■ 1400 Hubbell Place 1103 ■ (206) 232-2799 ■ www.seattlesuite. com ■ $

Reserving an affordable executive suite downtown provides upscale alternative accommodation. Each apartment here is fully furnished, and many offer fabulous city views. Enjoy complimentary Starbucks coffee and a games room with a pool table. Weekly and monthly rates are available; the minimum stay is three nights.

Chelsea Station Inn

MAP D2 ■ 4915 Linden Ave N ■ (206) 547-6077 ■ www.chelseastationinn. com ■ $$

This inn offers four large suites and access to 24-hour snacks. It is next to the south entrance of Woodland Park Zoo and just a short walk to Green Lake.

Budget Hotels and Hostels

American Hotel

MAP L6 ■ 520 South King Street ■ (206) 622-5443 ■ www.americanhotel seattle.com ■ $

Located in the heart of the International District, this is close to the transit and great cheap eateries. Choose from private rooms, some with their own tubs, or hotel style bunks. There are shared kitchen and social spaces.

City Hostel Seattle

MAP H3 ■ 2327 2nd Ave ■ (206) 706-3255 ■ www. hostelseattle.com ■ $

Award-winning budget accommodation sets this hostel above the rest, and it is just a short walk from most tourist attractions. Local artists display their work on the walls, and movie-makers show films in the small theater. The price includes breakfast, and the use of Wi-Fi.

The Maxwell Hotel Seattle

MAP H1 ■ 300 Roy St ■ (866) 866-7977 ■ www. themaxwellhotel.com ■ $

A locally owned hotel at the base of Queen Anne Hill, adjacent to the Space Needle. The Maxwell has spacious rooms, an indoor pool, free bicycle use, and free parking.

Moore Hotel

MAP J4 ■ 1926 2nd Ave ■ 1-800-421-5508 ■ No air conditioning ■ www. moorehotel.com ■ $

This hotel has simple, comfortable rooms, some with shared bathrooms. It enjoys a great location close to the Pike Place Market.

Panama Hotel

MAP L6 ■ 605 S Main St ■ (206) 223-9242 ■ No air conditioning ■ www. panamahotelseattle.com ■ $

Sabro Ozasa, a Japanese architect and University of Washington graduate, built this hotel in 1910. Since then, it has housed Japanese immigrants, Alaskan fisherman, and international travelers. Rooms have sinks only, but shared bathrooms have clawfoot tubs. The staff is multilingual.

Travelodge Seattle Center

MAP J2 ■ 200 6th Ave N ■ (206) 441-7878 ■ www. travelodge.com ■ $

Located near the Space Needle, this motel offers comfortable rooms, in-room coffee, and free local calls. Amenities are few, but there is a children's play area, free Continental breakfast, an outdoor pool, and parking.

University Motel Suites

MAP E2 ■ 4731 12th Ave NE ■ (206) 522-4724 ■ www.universitymotel suites.com ■ $

This budget option is just a few blocks from the I-5, so downtown is a quick drive away. Small suites have a living and kitchen area, a bedroom, and a full tub. There is free HBO and parking, plus laundry facilities.

Warwick Seattle Hotel

MAP J3 ■ 401 Lenora St ■ (206) 443-4300 ■ www. warwickwa.com ■ $

This hotel is a first-rate choice for travelers who want basic amenities at much lower prices. On top of many 24-hour extras – such as room service, business and gym, and courtesy van for anywhere within 2 miles (3 km) – there are rooms trimmed in fine woods and marble.

For a key to hotel price categories see p116

Index

Acknowledgments

Author
Eric Amrine

Additional contributor
Pam Mandel

Publishing Director Georgina Dee

Publisher Vivien Antwi

Design Director Phil Ormerod

Editorial Sophie Adam, Ankita Awasthi Tröger, Alice Fewery, Rachel Fox, Freddie Marriage, Alison McGill, Sally Schafer, Hollie Teague

Design Tessa Bindloss, Bhavika Mathur, Ankita Sharma

Cover Design Richard Czapnik

Commissioned Photography Scott Pitts

Picture Research Susie Peachey, Ellen Root, Lucy Sienkowska

Cartography Suresh Kumar, James Macdonald, Alok Pathak, Reetu Pandey

DTP Jason Little

Production Luca Bazzoli

Factchecker Carolyn Patten

Proofreader Laura Walker

Indexer Helen Peters

Picture Credits

Pretty Parlor: 83t.

Red Door Seattle: Brendan Boden 95br.

Robert Harding Picture Library: Richard Cummins 10clb.

Seattle Aquarium: Kevin Cruff 16cra.

Seattle Art Museum: 38b; Echo by Jaume Plensa Seattle Olympic Sculpture Park / Benjamin Benschneider 17tl.

Seattle Children's Theatre: Denny Sternstein 14cla.

Seattle Farmers Market Association: 99tl.

Seattle Great Wheel: 71tr, Vincent Yee 10crb.

Seattle Monorail: Megan Ching 72b.

Seattle Parks and Recreation: 4cla, 103br, 104b, 105cla; Discovery Park Nature Preschool Staff 33tl; Futoshi Kobayashi 25br; Laurel Mercury 46clb; TIA International Photography 11b, 32–3, 33cr, 33bl, 44cla, 47cra, 90tr.

Seattle Theatre Group: Bob Cerelli 42tl, 43tr.

Seattle's Best Tea: 22bl.

Sell Your Sole Consignment Boutique: Erica Sciareta 75cra.

Stoneburner: Geoffrey Smith 101crb.

Unicorn: Christopher Eltrich 11tl, 24–5, 79tl.

University of Washington Botanic Gardens: Copyright Stephanie Colony 58tl.

University Village: Lara Swimmer 56tr.

Victrola Coffee: 84t.

The Walrus and the Carpenter: Aaron Leitz 55bl.

Wing Luke Museum: Alabastro Photography 22cla.

Woodland Park Zoo: Dennis Dow 7br, 30cra, 31tl, 31crb; Ryan Hawk 30bl; Jeremy Dwyer-Lindgren 11cb, 31clb.

Cover

Front and spine: **Getty Images:** Artie Photography (Artie Ng)

Back: **Dreamstime.com:** Dhilde

Pull Out Map Cover

Getty Images: Artie Photography (Artie Ng)

All other images © Dorling Kindersley

For further information see: www.dkimages.com

As a guide to abbreviations in visitor information blocks: **Adm** = admission charge; **D** = dinner; **L** = lunch.

Penguin Random House

Printed and bound in China

First published in Great Britain in 2005 by Dorling Kindersley Limited 80 Strand, London WC2R 0RL

Copyright 2005, 2018 © Dorling Kindersley Limited

A Penguin Random House Company

18 19 20 21 10 9 8 7 6 5 4 3 2 1

Reprinted with revisions 2007, 2009, 2011, 2013, 2015, 2018

A CIP catalogue record is available from the British Library.

ISBN 978 0 2412 9663 9

MIX
Paper from responsible sources
FSC™ C018179

SPECIAL EDITIONS OF DK TRAVEL GUIDES

DK Travel Guides can be purchased in bulk quantities at discounted prices for use in promotions or as premiums. We are also able to offer special editions and personalized jackets, corporate imprints, and excerpts from all of our books, tailored specifically to meet your own needs.

To find out more, please contact:

in the US
specialsales@dk.com

in the UK
travelguides@uk.dk.com

in Canada
specialmarkets@dk.com

in Australia
penguincorporatesales@penguinrandomhouse.com.au

Selected Street Index